D1166885

THE ESSENTIALS OF FABULOUS

Because **Whatever** ***Doesn't Work Here Anymore***

ELLEN LUBIN-SHERMAN

ILLUSTRATED BY SUSAN SUGAR

2010

Ellen Lubin-Sherman is an executive coach with expertise in creating the visuals and the relationships that are the essential ingredients behind successful people and their businesses.

Printed in the United States of America

15 14 13 12 11 10   1 2 3 4 5

ISBN: 978-0-615-41503-1

Library of Congress Control Number: 2010915869

Illustrations by Susan Sugar.

This book is printed on paper made with 10% post-consumer recycled fiber and earning the Forest Stewardship Council (FSC) Certification.

To my North Stars,

Eddy L. Niceley and Harvey L. White,

in gratitude.

Contents

919

Preface

Count your lucky stars if you grew up without one illustrious relative to your name. That means you aren't under the delusion that you've inherited some magical gene or magnificent bankroll that makes you fabulous. It also means that you may be in on a secret: No one is born fabulous.

If you want to be fabulous, you have to *decide* to do it—to transform yourself into one of those amazing creatures that infiltrate our lives and ignite our dreams with their swagger, energy, pizzazz, and soigné charm.

Decided? Good. I'm going to help you do it. Why me? Here's why:

My early days had not a whit of excitement. I grew up in Brooklyn in the '60s. Went to the local public schools,

During the summer, we waited on the stoop for the chimes of the ice cream truck. A Fudgsicle was 25 cents, and you had to have your money ready or the truck would rumble down the street.

roller-skated in the street. I wasn't rich or well connected or a superstar in the classroom—but I figured out very early that it took moxie and verve to get things done, and I used that to great success. If I could find my pink diary with the official-looking "lock," I'm sure I would find, "If only Joni would have worn . . . " in the pages, because even at the age of eleven, I was a stealth stylist for my classmates. By the time I got to high school, I had discovered *Joyce Leslie,* a Kennedy/Johnson-era version of H&M, and was living it up in the knock-offs of more stylish pieces seen in fashion magazines. In my twenties, married and living in New York City, I took up competitive dressing instead of tennis, and spent my energy mastering a more-dash-than-cash look while polishing the perfect manners and business etiquette that I suspected would get me the corner office on the 16th floor. (It did.)

By my thirties, I was in the "all the things I'm supposed to do" mode—babies, suburbia, pursuing an ambitious communications career, and making the great discovery (equivalent to Galileo's?) that even if you weren't blessed with money, beauty, or connections, you could still go very far—*if you were fabulous.* Fabulous wasn't something you were born into; no, it was something you *became,* by keen observation, diligent application, and practice.

Over the years, I have changed careers, widened my networks, and kept "fabulous" as a near-constant goal because it has kept me relevant even as the grey hairs grew in. Maybe that's why I have never suffered from existential angst, save perhaps the angst of finding out my supplier of white cotton shirts has gone belly up.

I am one of those people who groove (and obsess) about the details, whether it's about heel height, a round or pointy toe cap, the subject line of an e-mail, or the importance of sending a thank-you note. On these things, I have an opinion and I'm not afraid to air it. I also have an expert eye for excellence, both in people and in behavior. I adore excellence. I swoon for competence. I'm in the tank for seemingly effortless and uncontrived fabulousness. Of course, *I* wasn't born fabulous. Are you kidding? No one is.

I've been writing and talking about fabulous (and its impact) for the last twenty-five years. My background is in launching luxury consumer products onto the marketplace. I understand the importance of packaging and how it impacts a product's success. So when I went looking for a new mountain to climb, someone suggested executive coaching with an expertise in self-marketing. Instead of packaging a product, I would help people package their persona. It matters—because if you don't have an image that's distinctive and memorable, you are going to be left in the dust.

As my coaching practice grew, I kept meeting terrific individuals who, for one reason or another, didn't know some basic truths about reputation—particularly that having a stellar one would protect them when times got tough. They were too casual about things you cannot be casual about, like full presence or exuding brio or saying your name slowly and clearly when you leave a voicemail message. They had the aptitude but not the attitude—the kind of *savoir "flair"* that is the very definition of you-know-what.

Upon launching my Web site, www.launchforward.com, I began writing a monthly column on professional excellence. I wrote about the basics—thank-you notes, showing up on time, polishing your shoes—and the not-so-basics, like warming up an e-mail, the hows and whys of positive self-talk, and the need to express enthusiasm for what you're doing. I was writing for anyone who wishes they had that extra little thing that could set them apart from the competition but didn't know where to start: new graduates trying to get a pinky in the door; executives returning to work after a hiatus; people who had lost their mojo and needed someone to tell them, "Just pick up the phone and invite that pooh-bah for lunch."

I've read hundreds of books on style, presentation, etiquette, and image, but when I've looked for a comprehensive guide to *fabulous*—one that tells you about all of those details that launch a person to the top—I couldn't find one. So, I've written the book myself. I'm quite convinced that being fabulous matters now more than ever because the game has changed. We've become so virtual that we're all walking around in a fog, tuned out to the world around us.

For most every job opening, there are hundreds of applicants, and more often than not, that pile of resumés is a big blur of sameness. To get ours to the top of the pile, we must know how to set ourselves apart, and that will take more than neat design and good writing. Our cover letter must capture the reader's attention in the first paragraph. But before that, we need to find the person making the hiring decision, and we do that by going to our database and seeing if someone has a connection to the company. Our e-mails to that person must be breathtakingly good—no, make that superior—so that we're instantly branded as a superperformer worth meeting. When we get that interview, we must show up on time, looking swank. Our handshake must be firm. And that's not all. Our thank-you note afterward must be sent within three days and include some relevant information that will demonstrate your first-rate intelligence and manners.

We've gotten so used to virtual interactions that when we have the opportunity to meet someone face to face, our communications have become sloppy, haphazard, or worse.

The choice is stark: Either we're the best we can be at all times or we risk being marginalized or, God forbid, tossed overboard. Let's admit it: We've developed some terrible habits that can easily derail even the most promising of trajectories.

A couple of months after launching my blog, "The Third Paragraph" (named in honor of my beloved aunt, who begged me to skip the drivel and get right to the juicy part of the letter), I received an e-mail from a woman who asked, "Do you have a book? I'd love to read you in a longer form." I wavered for about 15 seconds (me, write a book about being fabulous?) and then decided, *why not?* So here it is, a highly opinionated guide to becoming the absolute mostest, not because you're thin or once clerked for a judge, but because you're the whole exciting package: a connoisseur of people, an acquirer of friendships, and most importantly, unabashedly enthusiastic about living a fun-loving, upbeat-spouting, give-it-everything-you've-got kind of life.

Join me in this pursuit of the fabulous, wherever it might be. Let's be on the lookout for those moments when someone or something stops us in our tracks and makes us realize we've experienced the true, authentic thing: **the Fabulous One**. It could be a child of nine with impeccable manners or a woman of ninety who invites you into her home and offers you a cup of tea. No arrogance, no bluster, just the goodness of someone or something that's uncompromisingly superb.

The crazy thing is that you don't have to climb a mountain or sweep the ocean floor in order to find fabulous. It's right in front of you every day. Sometimes it's even inside *you*. Let's get it out. Come, I'll show you how.

Acknowledgments

I've been told that no one reads acknowledgments, but I would be remiss if I did not tell some extraordinary people how much their love and support meant to me as I wrote this book.

First I want to thank my Aunt Eddy, who not only loved me but thought she saw a glimmer of talent. Thank you, dear Aunt, for pointing out that my letters from camp were dull and ordinary until I got to the third paragraph. She taught me to get right to the point, and that's a rule I've lived by since I was 10. I'd also like to thank Gladys Bernstein, who gave me an A in an English class at Midwood High School in Brooklyn and wrote in the margin, "You are a writer." I remember staring at those words for a long, long time and feeling exultant by the praise of this most exacting teacher.

Jay T. Harris, my professor at the Medill School of Journalism in 1976, set me on my way, too, when he read one of my essays and told me I had talent but could never be a serious writer until I went out and lived a life. I know what he meant:

Go live outside the bubble I'd been living in. Thank you, Professor Harris, for making me challenge myself.

The Editrix, also known as Susan Gedutis Lindsay, came into my life in 2009 when I realized that I needed someone to guide me or, if you will, help me "birth the baby" that was inside of me. The Editrix first served as doula—mopping the brow, cheering me on, convincing me I could do it—then changed gears and became the editor's editor. There is no way I could have written this book without her. My three peer reviewers were also essential to the editing process, punching up the copy, waving the pompoms but also pointing out mystifying references, superfluous metaphors, and haughty and condescending commentary—and convincing me to delete the lines that only New Yorkers wouldn't be offended by. (Those lines will reappear in book number 2, so hang on, people.)

To Megan Verdugo, the extraordinary designer who materialized out of nowhere and took the book and ran with it, my deepest thanks and appreciation for the elegance of your work, the joy you take in the process, and above all, your marvelous attitude. I also wish to thank designer Shawn Girsberger, who was gracious enough to offer advice and resources. The decision to ask Susan Sugar to illustrate the book was a stroke of genius—her work is witty, clever, and extremely rich with detail. Known for her large oils and watercolors, Susan was unafraid to try something she had never done before and, boy, did she hit a bullseye.

Lori Windolf Crispo, you, my dear, are what's known as a foxhole buddy (except you're attired in pearls and smart pantsuits). I'd want you in the trenches with me always. To Marina Crispo: Only a screenwriter like Billy Wilder could have invented you. You are like no other—an amazing combination of wit, passion, and flawless style. It is no wonder that everyone wants to be on your radar screen. Thank you, Marina, for everything you've done.

Friends and board members—Suzanne Falk, Pamela Massenburg, Shelley Niceley-Groff, Kristina Drinkwine, Linda and Harold Yaffe, Toni and Ray Maloney, Susan Wolfson, Robin Sanders, Deborah Lerner Duane, Nicole Tatz, Carey Graeber, Connie Castellan, Jody MacWright, Eva Gentry, Jiang Ni, and Dana Caputo—thank you for your unstinting support and unswerving confidence. I never asked you to schlep the espresso machine but I know you would have done it.

And finally, to my beloved parents and the über-fabulous Sherman "boys," Mark, Alexander, and Joshua. For years, you listened while I talked about writing a book, but never harangued or said, "Just do it already!" Thank you for believing in me and not letting me give up. Your joy in seeing me succeed is all I ever dreamed about.

Introduction

What, me? Fabulous?

Ever wonder how some people make it all look so *easy*? They walk into a party and unhesitatingly initiate an introduction to a stranger. They exude confidence and style. They dazzle us with their humor and accessibility. They look like a million bucks even in a downpour. And they keep smiling. They are *fabulous.*

We know fabulous when we see it. It's a thunderbolt—a moment so seismic we feel as if we've been lifted off the ground. The people who loom large in our minds, whose high spirits bring the oxygen back into the room, whose playful natures inspire us to have more fun, and who can wind a few strands of apparent junk around their necks and still look mind-bogglingly stunning—they are unforgettable. (And don't think they don't know it, either.)

I know what happens to me when I'm with someone who's not only terrific at what they do but also terrifically nice and warm: I *swoon.* How can I spend more time with her? Maybe we can work together? Perhaps she needs some pencils sharpened? I certainly want to take one (or two or five) of her fabulous characteristics and make them part of my repertoire. She seems to *have it all*—great manners, a dazzling presence, a defined sense of self—and she is completely original.

What makes her so fabulous? Well, fabulous is a strategy. A viewpoint. An attitude about life. It's chain-mail armor, discipline, and a commitment to being generous and open, straightforward and real. It's about loving yourself, believing in your abilities, and then going after everything you want without compromising on manners, good taste, ethics, and charm. It's about being resilient **and** having fun, no matter how many curve-balls life throws at you.

Why be fabulous?

Look, you've probably read the how-to books and guides in hopes of finding out how to go from being "fine" (*yawn*) to *gaga* (*gasp!*). But here's some news: You're never going to find what you're looking for in those recycled stories because the truth is (are you ready?) . . . unless you love yourself, find yourself amusing, get a kick out of yourself, enjoy spending time in your own company . . . unless you truly believe you're enchanting, you can never project "fabulous," no matter what the books tell you.

And here's something else you need to know: You don't have to be younger or look thinner or taller or have more money or a *pied-à-terre* in the West Village (although that is kinda fabulous) to be fabulous. In fact, some of the most fabulous people in the world are short, squat, and sport threadbare pants with mismatched jackets (and *do* have *pied-à-terres* in the West Village!) but what makes them extraordinary is the way you feel when you're in their air. It's that fresh and bracing.

Can you remember the last time you wore something ever-so-slightly outlandish, like a pair of purple stockings with fire-engine red patent leather pumps or an after-5 hat with a black net over your face, and delighted in your audacity and wit? Have you ever walked into a cocktail party and immediately introduced yourself to the most fabulous-looking couple in the room and then moved on to the next most fabulous couple in the room and by the end of the night you had talked to everyone at the party and realized, maybe on the way home, that it was in fact YOU who was the most fabulous person in the room? No? Would you like to?

You want to be irresistible? You will be. You want more pizzazz? No problem-o. Together we'll get you to the point where you're supremely confident and serenely adept at being you at your finest, your best, your most terrific self.

But first you have to forget what the beauty magazines tell you. No one looks better because of lasers, fillers, scrubs, creams, ointments, salves, gels, or moisturizers. The only antidote to getting crepey is *attitude*—an amazing and life-affirming attitude toward yourself and the people around you. This is what makes people ageless. And get this: When you're fabulous you will never have to worry about wrinkles. They'll be irrelevant.

You also will never worry about being alone, not only because your personal energy is a gravitational pull to other remarkable people but because you will always have the company of someone wonderful: **you**. You know those people who are always talking on their cell phones? They are not fabulous. Fabulous people are content to walk and think and observe and luxuriate in their heads. The steady stream of chatter between their ears is upbeat . . . who needs to listen to complaints, narcissistic rants, and obnoxious commentary when they can take themselves out for a divine tuna fish sandwich and listen to that all-talk radio show inside their head, dreaming up ideas, deconstructing novels, shopping their closet, planning parties, arguing with neighbors, telling off their boss, or whatever it is they do when they're in that wonderful head of theirs.

Back in the old days (when "To the moon, Alice!" from *The Honeymooners* was the expression *du jour*), we likened life to a merry-go-round. You know . . . get on a horse and try to grab the brass ring. Sounds quaint, no? Today, life is not about riding in a circle. It's about trajectory, boosted by your winning attitude and headed for the stratosphere. But: Only. If. You're **fabulous**.

Let's get started but let's not take forever to do it because the world is hungry for fabulous. And the world is hungry for you!

The Ten-Plus Traits of the Truly and Completely Fabulous

I've spent years thinking about what it means to be fabulous. As I've said, there are a thousand things that make someone fabulous. Yet, I do believe that fabulous can be narrowed down to eleven primary qualities, and here they are.

1. They are passionate about life.

2. They are delightfully authentic.

3. They are revered for their amazing attitude.

4. They are warm and completely accessible.

5. They have flair.

6. They have impeccable manners.
7. They're competent.
8. They just "get it."
9. They have a big bandwidth.
10. They are vivid virtually.
11. They have a board.

Each chapter covers one of these eleven items, in order. I've laid out each chapter so that it's very clear to see the skills you need to master each of the competencies that define "fabulous." Along with the bossy suggestions and heartfelt entreaties, I've also included useful tips that are the crib notes to being fabulous. I assure you—no one else is gonna tell you this stuff.

So start reading and see how it applies to the life you're leading. It's a cliché but true: Life is a process. No one takes the express lane to Fabulous . . . this is a 10-items-plus venture. I've left room so you can make notes to yourself about what you need to work on and if I've referred to a book, I've listed that book in the appendix so you can add it to your library.

Stop fretting. It won't take forever. I promise.

Fabulous people are passionate about life.

1

For me, the road to fabulous starts at passion. Why? Because passion is the life force, the very heart of fabulous. It is the rocket booster. It is the lustiness that drives us all batty, with plans and dreams and roads taken (and *not* taken . . . but by conscious choice). Fabulous people are passion incarnate.

With passion, life is an adventure, an open landscape filled with possibilities. There is never a dull moment, since the dull moments are always being transformed into options to be explored. You must not underestimate its power. It can change your life.

Everyone's passion is different. How can you find yours? You must first figure out what makes you tick, what makes you swoon with excitement. And then when you've figured that out, you must throw caution to the wind and go after your heart's desire. Do it! Don't ask permission from anybody, don't second-guess yourself, just go, go, go! This takes courage, energy, drive, and ambition. But the payoff? The payoff is a life filled with amazing adventures and unlimited trajectories.

WHERE TO START:

Passion is made up of many things, but its raw power comes from knowing what you love in life and then going out and living it. What have the passionate got that makes them the life of every party?

- They breathe oxygen into the room with their lusty, seemingly inexhaustible energy.
- They understand what they like and what they don't like, and they're also very smart about what they're good at.
- They are expert optimists—looking at the world and finding the fun in the quotidian.
- They are always creating new ways to make their lives rich with excitement.
- They are fascinated by everything (except maybe arithmetic).
- They aren't worried about what people think, so they're free to be themselves at all times.
- They get a kick out of champagne and figs and discovering that Woolite now makes an "Extra Dark" edition to keep their black pants from fading.
- They have the courage and the guts to go after everything they desire.

Whoa . . . let me back up just a bit. Let's take a closer look at these, one at a time.

They are full of (seemingly) inexhaustible energy.

I am not going to lie to you—this is it, the unmistakable mark of the truly and utterly fabulous: energy! Some call it pizzazz; others might term it "caffeinated." I'm talking about a bubbly, high-spirited—fine, let's call it *lusty*—appetite for living . . . that's how passionate people operate on a daily basis. Wanna know the reason they can do this? They've figured out one of life's greatest secrets: Put work and play together, and every day becomes a terrific adventure. It's no wonder that these passionate wunderkinds are unstoppable—they're grooving on their own delicious euphoria!

This is what work is supposed to feel like: a combination of passion, enthusiasm, and love for whatever you do. If it's anything less than that, make a change, figure it out, ask for help—but never stop reaching for that kind of complete engagement that only happens when you're completely enmeshed and head over heels with your life's passion.

It is true that even the most passionate lose their mojo and need to retreat from the action every now and then. But I assure you . . . their recovery time is short because they love their lives too much. They love the action, the tumult, and the controlled chaos of living their lives to the fullest. And when the blues hit or the energy flags, they don't mess around—they're not about to let a temporary glitch ruin that gorgeous indomitable spirit. They go back to the basics: eating three meals a day, going to sleep at a sensible hour, listening to music, buying a pair of peep-toe pumps, volunteering, and exercising—because, let's face it, passion is what defines them, what makes them memorable, and they cannot afford to be infected with the glum-and-bored virus.

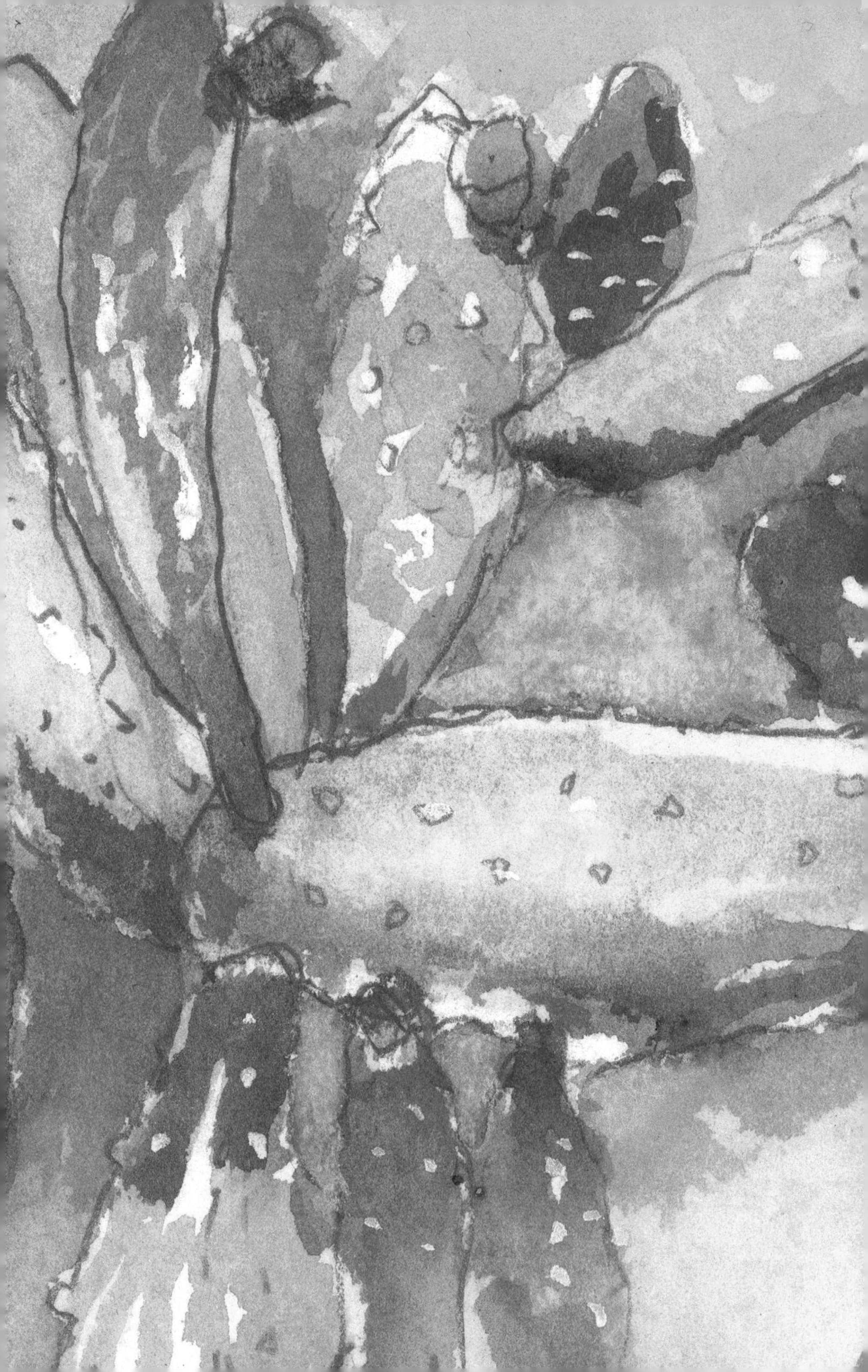

They know what makes them tick.

Maybe you were one of the lucky ones. Maybe somewhere along the way someone took you aside and told you that you were gifted, that you had a talent for something—writing, cooking, relationships, fashion, sales, computer programming. Or maybe you figured it out for yourself. Or maybe you're still trying to figure out just exactly what you ought to be doing with your talents and skills. It's okay. Be patient with yourself, because they don't teach self-knowledge in college. You need to figure it out yourself. And figure it out you *must,* because this is the secret of a happy and passionate life: You identify your gift and you incorporate that gift into your daily life. You take this remarkable quality that makes you a standout and you name it, and then you showboat it.

Let's say you're "easy to be with." (What a fabulous quality!) Now, throughout the day, telegraph the fact you're easy to be with, by being easy to be with. Begin every day with a cheery hello. Leave your door open at work so people can walk in and ask you a question. Offer to mentor someone in your company. Smile at people and look them in the eye when you speak to them. Send upbeat and motivating e-mails to your staff and your friends.

Forget about all the things you're lousy at. Not rich? Mismatched furniture? Not driving a Porsche? No one cares. Keep the focus on the positive—*your* positive. Just do what

Those who deride and undermine your confidence are prickly pears. It is wise to avoid them.

you love (you love being with others, so you're easy to be with) and love what you do, so that nothing impedes your sense of involvement and satisfaction. It will be its own reward.

They prefer optimism.

Even the most optimistic among us will tell you: It's not easy to stay upbeat. *Mon Dieu!* Most of the time it feels as if we're walking through a desert trying to avoid getting pricked by a pear cactus. But the optimistic know that the ability to see the good over the bad will outsmart the negative types who are remarkably gifted at pointing out everything that's *wrong* with the world (and with you!) and the few things that are *right*. To stay upbeat, you must rid yourself of anyone or anything that can send you running for the cave (or the Witness Protection Program).

. . . Which is why they stay away from pessimists and "frenemies."

Some say the scourge of mankind is loneliness. No question—but that doesn't mean you should fill the void by spending time with people who are mean spirited, who take pleasure in pointing out your blind spots. Surround yourself with people who genuinely love you, inspire you, and want you to succeed. That's important because right up there with loneliness is the temptation to submit to self-doubt. Nothing knocks us off our stride faster than a negative friend, or worse, a deriding voice inside our head putting fear into our every move.

That's where the passionate shine—they take the praise they've acquired over the years and upload it to their personal soundtrack. Over and over they are listening to this magnificent stream of affirming commentary, a mélange of whatever their best friend/fourth-grade teacher/the boss who recognized that they had talent *and had to do something with it* told them, so they could move forward in their lives with brio. And by the way, this is also the secret of confidence: listening to the words of the people who see what's wonderful in you and allowing them to rewrite the self-doubting, self-castigating **nonsense** you've bought into.

Now I know it's easy to say and not so easy to do. How exactly do you get rid of what I call "superpredators"—those who pose as dear friends but never act in your best interest? The only answer: *Just do it.* Don't play games, don't be coy. Deal with the problem honestly and directly. Tell them the relationship is not working and wish them well. And then stop calling them back. It's not easy to say good-bye to a friendship but it's necessary when the friendship becomes a battleground for unresolved feelings of jealousy, envy, or just plain hurtfulness.

Does it seem overwhelming, maybe even harsh, to say good-bye to a friendship that's gone sour? Trust me, it's not. It's clarifying and uplifting, because now you will have more time to spend with the people who think you're the cat's meow. You know I'm right: Just delete their name and numbers from your cell phone. *Bravo!*

Of course, becoming and staying optimistic is not just about shedding friends. It's about attracting them, too. You know how it is . . . you're invited to a dinner, ready to have fun, meet someone new. But when you get there, you find yourself seated next to the stealth BlackBerry-man, who pretends to engage in conversation while keeping his eye (and thumbs) on his beloved smartphone. Clearly you guys are *not going to have Paris.* Change seats!

On the other hand, having developed this remarkable *joie de vivre,* you seek out the stimulating and compelling people, and you will discover that they find you equally beguiling. Coincidence? I think not. Passionate people do not intimidate equally exciting and dynamic people with their force-of-nature personalities and extraordinary *bonhomie.*

There's the choice: Tingle with excitement and hobnob with like-minded souls, or spend time with people who compare kitchen renovations and the benefits of going all organic. (So *virtuous.*) Take your pick. One way to start tingling is to start taking care of yourself. That helps you to stay positive, and it creates a charged force field around you, a magnet that attracts other exciting people. Indulge in the things that bring you pleasure and hopefulness, including: adequate sleep, healthy diet, friendships, relationships, books, movies, or whatever puts a spring in your step. You must constantly remind yourself of the joy and pleasure you bring to the people who surround you. Laugh every day, at least four times a day, because nothing is as musical or as seductive as hearing someone not merely *living* but *loving* their life.

They are always in the throes of creating and producing.

Passion and its ability to keep you feeling mobilized and productive can never be taken for granted. This magnificent gift must be protected and nourished by a steady diet of big and challenging goals, meaningful work, interesting friends, and happiness-inducing activities that keep you feeling empowered and consequential. Look for opportunities to grow, to learn, to stretch—even to fail. And always say "yes" to things that might at first strike you as silly or nonsensical.

How to Spot a Frenemy

fren·e·my (fr n' -m) n. pl. **fren·e·mies** Informal. A person who pretends to be a friend but is actually an enemy; a rival with which one maintains friendly relations. (**dictionary.com**)

- You mention in a phone call that you're working on a new project and Frenemy's first response is to change the subject.
- You continue talking about the new project and Frenemy suddenly has to take an incoming call (and never calls back to continue the conversation).
- You get a new hairstyle and Frenemy says, "Did you get a haircut?" and then doesn't comment.
- You've been invited to Frenemy's house for dinner. Frenemy knows you're a vegetarian. Alas, there are no vegetables on the menu. Frenemy tells you, "I have a good friend who became a vegetarian and her complexion has gone completely gray."
- You're about to celebrate a birthday that ends in zero. You mention to your Frenemy that you're starting to feel "old." The next time you see Frenemy she looks at you sympathetically and says, "You know what? You *are* starting to look old."
- You are between jobs. Frenemy repeatedly talks about someone else's successes.
- You're looking for freelance work. Frenemy leaves you a voicemail message saying, "Call me fast. I may have a lead for you." You call her. And call her. And call her. Two weeks later she returns your phone call and doesn't remember the lead.
- Your husband has taken a new job that involves commuting. You tell Frenemy that you don't think it will impact the closeness in your marriage. Frenemy responds, "I had a friend whose husband commuted and within a year he was cheating."

It's possible that you'll have the time of your life, and your playful nature will get a refresher course in feeling as giddy as a baby in a swing.

They are not afraid to try something new.

Few people will ever pat you on the back and say, "Wow, you're great. You're so curious." But they ought to—especially if you are always on the lookout for the new *new* . . . cheese, vacation spot, food, or author. The ability to get up in the morning and be perpetually fascinated by the world is the high-octane gas behind the truly passionate.

This is what drives them: an insatiable interest in being stimulated, provoked, amused, and, most importantly, engaged. Whether it's by reading, travel, or perfecting a new skill like knitting or French, the curious among us who take pleasure in the new are always going to be the incandescent bulbs that illuminate others' lives.

They are a force.

Like a white-noise machine that blocks out the sound of voices, the interior monologue of the passionate, with its emphasis on self-acceptance and purposeful activities, can neutralize the ever-present voices of gloom, doom, and fear that can sabotage anyone's efforts. Everyone has doubt; it's just that some choose to block it out and move forward anyway. They bank on passion's tensile strength and its byproduct, optimism, to move them through the bad days when a small rock can sometimes seem as immoveable as a Stonehenge boulder. (The passionate remember that someone moved those Stonehenge blocks there in the first place.)

The thing is, those wary voices in our heads are there for a reason, of course: to protect us. No one wants to make a mistake, but the biggest mistake of all is playing it so safe that you forget what the frisson of risk-taking feels like. If you're looking to add a little passion to your salad, toss in a jalapeno, not a cucumber. You've got to throw yourself into something—anything!—with the same kind of irrational blindness that makes you fall in love. Tell yourself that no one and nothing is gonna stop you. Approach your life the way a mountaineer approaches the world's highest mountains: In making the trek they know not to look up (too daunting) and not to look down (too paralyzing). They look straight ahead, making the climb one step at a time. It's as good a rule for mountain climbers as it is for the rest of us climbing our personal Mt. Kilimanjaros.

They are never blasé.

How easy it might be to dismiss the joyful, childlike enthusiasms of the truly passionate. After all, how can anyone who takes herself seriously get euphoric over a Uni-ball 0.5 Signo pen from Japan (www.jetpens.com)? But that's the secret: The passionate don't take themselves too seriously. (Can you imagine?) Yes, they take their work seriously. They take their relationships seriously. They raise children that, as Fran Lebowitz so brilliantly put it, "you can sit next to on an airplane." Still, they never lose the excitement of stumbling upon new delights.

That's how the passionate persevere. That is how they fight the temptation to submit to boredom, exhaustion, and hopelessness. They deliberately block out the noise of negativity and despair and keep their eyes on the big prize they're hankering for. Don't you see? The big stuff—the vacations,

They Asked for It

In her charming memoir, *D.V.*, legendary fashion editor Diana Vreeland recounts how she was awarded France's highest honor: "This is how I got the Légion d'honneur. I asked for it. I was told by someone quite reliable that you only get it if you ask for it, so I asked." (Reading this paragraph stopped me in my tracks. This wasn't chutzpah; this was brilliance!)

A friend of mine who was in the middle of finishing a documentary film about Afghanistan needed office space. If you know anything about documentaries, you know there's very little money to spare. So this clever lady called Columbia University in New York and asked if they would give her film company office space so they could edit the film. They gave it to her—*gratis*. (Again, brilliance!)

Dear readers, we know the moral to these two stories: Ask for things! Feel entitled! Be courageous! But advocating for ourselves is a challenge for many of us.

Before asking someone for help, we first need to do a little self-scrutiny. We need to weigh the risks and decide if the risks are worth it. Are you asking the right person? Do you have enough capital to make the request? Are you crossing a boundary line?

My formula for asking is this: If they say "yes," will my life be enhanced? If they say "no," will my ego be crushed to smithereens? We all know there are very few requests that could crush our egos to smithereens, so I try to err on the side of asking too much, rather than asking too little. Once you get the hang of it, it's quite freeing.

Why do I feel that most of us should ask more? Because I know that most people give more than they take. We give advice, support, connections, recommendations, strategic thinking, and then, when we need something in return, we worry and drag our feet, rather than pick up the phone and say, "I need . . . " or "I want . . . , " or "Can you please arrange . . . ?"

Permitting ourselves to ask for things is no simple skill. In fact, I think it's the most critical and undervalued component of the job search, of widening your social network, of moving ahead in your career. Everyone you're meeting with, having lunch with, working with knows at least ten other people. And those ten people might be helpful to you, but only if you ask for what you want.

For those of us who have spent our lives cowering rather than asking for the Légion d'honneur, some tips:

- Never ask a favor from someone who doesn't have the power or the wherewithal to dispense it.
- Asking is not to be confused with impertinence.
- No one has unlimited capital so don't presume that you can ask without giving back.
- Actors have auditions; athletes have tryouts. If you're stuck in a job search, identify a target company and ask to do a demonstration.
- Determine how much you want something—a new job, an introduction to a well-connected colleague or someone wonderful. Then decide if it's worth the risk of rejection to ask.
- Power is never given; you have to ask for it.
- Asking takes practice. Start with small favors and work your way up to big ones.
- Some people are afraid to ask because it's beneath them. Maybe . . . but it wasn't beneath Diana Vreeland, who wanted the red ribbon in her buttonhole—and who got it.

the new cars, the longed-for promotion—those big moments come around all too infrequently. You need to groove on all the little things—the pen with the perfect grip, two or three ranunculuses in a flea market bud vase, even a sunny day. And don't be afraid to show it.

They let it rip.

Do you wear your heart on your sleeve? Alas, there are still some people out there who haven't figured out how much fun it is to throw caution (and Mommy's admonishing words, *"Lower your voice!"*) to the wind. There are actually a few people left who think it's sophisticated to feign excitement rather than wallow in it. Listen to them at your peril. The blasé and jaded types are cowards. Their indifference is just a mask to protect them from failure or rejection.

What the passionate do better than most is let it rip. Since they're way, way past the point of worrying about fitting in or (God forbid) trying to please everyone, and since they know that no one is talking about them (since everyone is talking about themselves!), they don't have to waste a minute doing anything but what feels right. They put it all out there, wearing their zest and appetite like a *Légion d'honneur* medal. By listening to that caressing inner soundtrack urging them on to greater heights, they can take on the world (and if they miss the mark this time, they'll have another opportunity soon enough).

HOW TO DO IT?

My friends, take heart. We are not born with passion; we acquire it . . . like the measles. One day you're perfectly content to wear all shades of beige and then after a summer vacation visiting a brazenly fabulous cousin, there's no way you're sticking to earth tones. Ignited by her self-deprecating wit, curiosity, and glamour, you're inspired to follow suit. Awakened to the possibilities of reinvention, you acquire other wonderful habits, like introducing yourself to strangers, smiling easily, and becoming rather shamelessly profligate with compliments. With this marvelous attitude as your calling card, you find yourself completely intoxicated by the air you're emitting and its gravitational pull on other equally amusing and clever souls. Your passion for living is palpable and no one can resist you. Ah, happy days!

Now that you're on fire, you're getting things done. That's right—you're moving at a clip because the combination of courage, energy, and having a mission packs a pretty big wallop. With your crisp competence permanently on display, your passion can seduce even dithering types who might want to wait and see, rather than smartly move ahead and accomplish something. Picture the passionate as a tsunami: Run like hell or be swept up in their all-encompassing, force-to-be-reckoned-with wave.

The passionate start each day like an L.A. morning, filled with the sunny certainty that hard work, quiet drive, steely determination, and luck (of course!) will be enough to get the ball rolling. This talent—genius, really—for putting it all out there is perhaps the greatest lesson we can take from these astonishingly productive types: Take a risk, don't get distracted, take pleasure in outperforming the competition. Yes, of course people will be envious that you're consumed with passion for something you care deeply about. But, hey—you can't help yourself. (Lucky you.)

To develop passion:

1. **Determine what makes you tick.** Be attuned to the things you love, whether it's making a scrapbook or training for a marathon. Look around and study the people in your life who exude purpose and who love what they do. Listen when they talk about their interests and how it comes across as topical and interesting information that they're sharing, not braggadocio. Develop your own little spiel about your work and yourself, and practice it in the privacy of your bathroom (clear the vanity and practice in front of a mirror).
2. **Circumvent ennui and existential angst by tenaciously removing any negative influences from your force field.** Seek out the company of people who are engaging and energizing *and* who are equally besotted by you.
3. **Groove on yourself.** Don't be afraid to be different! And when things don't work out, don't blame yourself for failing; congratulate yourself for trying (because most people don't even do that). And when you figure out what you love to do, do it! Shout it from the rooftops! Someone who's passionate about living a purposeful life needs to infect as many people as possible.

RESOURCES

I reboot my own sense of passion by reading:

***The Principles of Uncertainty* by Maira Kalman**

Kalman, Maira. *The Principles of Uncertainty.*
New York: The Penguin Press, 2007.

The next time you hear someone whine, "There's nothing to do," I suggest you hand them Kalman's account of a day spent traveling to Brooklyn on the New York subway. By finding the fun in the everyday—purchasing a new ball of string for her string collection or grabbing a hot dog at Nathan's—Kalman is the perfect tour guide to seeing the world anew.

Life Is Short, Wear Your Party Pants by Loretta LaRoche

LaRoche, Loretta. *Life Is Short, Wear Your Party Pants.*
Carlsbad, CA: Hay House, Inc., 2003.

LaRoche is one of those believers who think that if you get up in the morning convinced that this is your day, it will be. From introducing yourself to someone on the checkout line to putting together an outfit that screams "rock star," LaRoche has a list of easy things to do to find the passion that's central to "an amazing life."

The Illustrated Woody Allen Reader by Woody Allen

Allen, Woody. *The Illustrated Woody Allen Reader.*
New York: Alfred A. Knopf, Inc., 1993.

What can I say? I'm a sucker for Woody Allen's sublimely ridiculous take on life. Just reading excerpts from his movies and monologues ("Your self-esteem is like a notch below Kafka's") makes me giggle, and giggling midday when the work and the world are whirling all around is terrifically uplifting and energizing.

D.V. by Diana Vreeland

Vreeland, Diana. *D.V.*
New York: Alfred A. Knopf, Inc., 1984.

It must have been pretty fabulous to be Diana Vreeland but it's also fabulous to see how she took her energies and passion for fashion and style and created a career that still inspires people with its originality and intelligence.

Fabulous people are delightfully authentic.

2

The omnipotent narrator inside our head intones, "Be thyself." We all know it's true. And yet, we waste precious time trying to be something we are not: pretending to be rushed when we're in dire need of a few words of friendship; projecting a supercilious front when we're too shy to initiate a hello; and the worst, behaving in an exclusionary manner because we're terrified to move outside our circle of comfort. Do I really need to tell you how fabulous it is to be real?

Authenticity is the sine qua non of everything that matters. When you encounter someone unguarded, without artifice or pretense—*Mon Dieu!*—you know it. I compare it to being at the top of the mountain: the air is clearer, there's nothing to muddy the senses. It's bracingly refreshing.

Authentic people are destined, some might say determined, to have more fun. They carry themselves with ease to invite closeness. They like themselves. How lucky they are to move through the day unhampered by a scolding interior voice depleting their energies. Their inner monologues produce a kind of unerring confidence that's inspiring and attainable.

WHERE TO START:

Make no mistake about it: The surest way to cut the widest swath is to let nothing distract from your completely authentic sense of self. No airs, no pretensions, just the presentation of one's self at one's best, all of the time.

What would our lives look like if we were totally and completely real? What can we learn from the fabulous about authenticity?

They are happy in their skin.

Let me ask you this: When was the last time you took yourself out on a date? No cell phone, no smartphone, no iPod, no computer—just you, alone in your thoughts and observations. Did you find yourself good company? Were you amused by the flotsam and jetsam floating around in your head? Did you finish your date thinking, "We should do this more often?" If you didn't immediately rebook, you are missing out on one of life's great discoveries: **you!**

There's a reason authentic people enjoy their own company. They're fun to be with! They've worked to ensure that their company is top notch. They do things that are offbeat and unexpected. They challenge themselves with big aspirations and lofty goals and they don't give up till they have reached them. (And when they let themselves down by treating people shabbily, they hold themselves accountable and try to resolve the situation as soon as possible.)

When you haven't figured out who you are and what you offer the world, it's awfully easy to get hoodwinked into thinking you're not as good as everyone else. It's even easier to start taking on the airs and pretensions of someone you're not. Don't bother. There's nothing fabulous about a generic. We always pay more for the original.

They are anti-phony.

Lord, have mercy. Do not send another smug or arrogant person to ruin my day. Rid me of these shrewish types who ride herd from atop their self-important perches. Lord, do not let me mimic their icy *hauteur* when I am writhing in misery because they are seated next to me, text messaging furiously, in the theater. Remind me there is goodness and graciousness in being unpretentious and humble, that not even Oprah Winfrey, who sits at No. 1 on *Forbes* magazine's Richest African-Americans list, seeks vengeance when she is locked out of the Hermes store in Paris at closing time.

The authentic do not walk among us armed and ready to go *mano a mano* lest anyone dare to question their authority. They do not need to bludgeon us with their accomplishments. No. They wear their success humbly, confident that just by being in their air space, we'll quickly figure out that they are the realest deal going. Watch them in action. Whether it's bantering with the waitress at the diner or making small talk with the guy at the car wash, the

There ain't nothing like the real thing, whether it's Coke, Motown, or you.

truly authentic are enormously gifted at putting everyone in the mood for fun.

To avoid and avert the contagion of the pretentious types, set your radar screen to detect and avoid incoming missiles of blowhard commentary and ostentatious flaunting. Treat these insecure types with the compassion they deserve and listen with only one ear while you mentally count the black pants in your closet.

They invite you in.

Authentic people get a kick out of being close. They savor relationships and they're not afraid of the icky part, which requires intimacy and honesty. Perhaps I should explain how the "icky" part works. It's like this: When you have a relationship with someone, you open yourself up, warts and all. You admit to mistakes. You share regrets. You dream aloud. You plot, you plan, you scheme, you conspire, and you do all of it with trust and confidence that you're not being judged. The truly authentic know that at their core they are very good, sometimes even fabulous. They also know that they are flawed and make the same idiotic mistakes that everyone else makes. So there's no shame in owning up to being an idiot . . . in fact, it's the owning up to being an idiot that puts them in the Fabulous pantheon.

This sharing of personal insufficiencies is remarkably moving, some might say humbling. But it is the only way to forge a bond of true intimacy and caring.

If you're unsure about whether you are capable of accessibility, think of how lonely you've felt in the presence of someone determined to keep you at arm's length. Think of how shallow the conversation has been when the truth has been sugarcoated and nothing of substance is shared. Now think about a moment when you've let down your guard, told the truth, and felt understood. Did it feel good? That's the goal.

They seduce you with their charm.

I'll admit it: I'm a sucker for brainy charm. I find those effervescently charming types, with their easy smiles, impeccable manners, and their transparent (and honest) love of life, simply irresistible. They make you feel as if you are the most important and interesting person in the room! And the way they can lift your spirits—remarkable! Could it be because they're happy with themselves? (If you haven't figured it out by now, here's a tip: Hang out with happy people.)

Charm's key ingredient is consideration for others. You demonstrate it with your manners. We're not talking finger bowls here (although if you're presented with a finger bowl, you should dip the tips of your fingers into the bowl, swish them around gently, and then dry them on the cloth provided . . . very nice). Impeccable manners (returning a phone call or e-mail; standing when someone enters the room; acknowledging and inviting someone to join you in conversation) will take you places you haven't even dreamed about. It's the one thing you can bank on when nothing else is working for you.

Charm is openness—someone who makes eye contact and does not look or care if someone more "important" walks into the room. Charm is warmth—an easy smile, being the first to say hello, remembering what someone told you the last time you met (and, if appropriate, asking a follow-up question such as, "How did that project work out?") Charm

How to Write a Love Note to Yourself

- Everyone should write themselves a veritable love note and tuck it in the wallet next to the emergency cash.
- This love note should not be filled with hyperbole or nonsense.
- However, it's okay to exaggerate a teensy bit, especially if you have literary capabilities.
- Tell the truth: What do you like about yourself?
- Write that down.
- Now pick up the phone and ask your closest, most trustworthy friend for your best qualities. (Ability to spot a Michael Kors skirt at a discount store does not make the cut.)
- Include intellectual as well as emotional competencies. Being lousy at math is definitely cancelled out by being a terrific guest at a party.
- Admit it: You're fun, you're humble, and you don't take things for granted.
- Dig deeper: You're very good at what you do and you're not afraid to challenge yourself by taking on new responsibilities.
- Come clean; this is about you. You're not a serial canceller. I said this was a "love" letter.

is listening when someone is speaking and indicating with your body that you're totally engaged. Charm is the ability to let someone grab all of your attention without feeling a need to talk about what *you* are doing.

Charm is full presence. You wouldn't consider checking a BlackBerry or answering a phone call when meeting or speaking with someone—friend, contact, colleague, or client! (Do you know how many deals have been soured because someone felt dismissed instead of appreciated by a BlackBerry-wielder?) You really want to win me over with charm? Notice me! Listen to what I'm saying so our conversation is mutually gratifying and energizing. Acknowledge a quality of mine that you admire and share it with me so that I walk away from the encounter feeling ten feet tall. Having the insight to know what people want and deserve, and then the confidence and courage to give it to them in spades, is another reason that charming people stand head and shoulders above the rest. This charm has at its core a deep and profound interest in other people's wellbeing. Who wouldn't be awed?

They are generous with themselves (and their smarts).

Let's face it, the fabulous are really, really smart, especially when it comes to what people need, and they know that everyone needs something. A name, a lead, a referral—a savvy accountant—we can all use something to make our lives easier and more fun. So why not share?

This is where nobody does it better than the fabulous, authentic types—they're happy to see other people get ahead because they're not threatened by it. And so, when they're listening to you speak, they're mentally riffling through their Black Book of people you need to know. They groove on setting up a lunch for the three of you or furnishing your resumé with a cover note testifying to your acumen and originality. They don't see it as going out of their way but just something that everyone ought to be doing just because it's right and nice. If you have a friend who's always pushing you to success, hold that friend with two hands, not one. (And, by the way, you do not need to have connections to house seats on Broadway to be considered generous. Just listening without saying "I could have told you that" is an enormous gift.)

The next time you're with a friend or a colleague and you spot a gap—a little spot where they could use some shoring up—ask if there's anything you can do to help. If the answer is "yes," don't wait. *Do it.*

They make you feel good.

Truly authentic types see life through a lens of humor and come armed with a smorgasbord of small-talk topics guaranteed to make you feel as if you're infinitely interesting. In their company, you can let your guard down. You can enjoy being with them because their very authenticity makes you feel better about the world. (*Pssst:* If you're having a chat and you're suddenly getting the heebie jeebies, it's not you! You are probably in the force field of someone wary about connecting on a meaningful [and that means honest] level.)

They are delightfully self-assured.

This unerring belief in one's own acceptability is nothing short of mind-blowing. Just try to imagine the energy behind your swing if every time you stepped up to the plate you believed you were Derek Jeter. Just think of the fun you would have if you started your day with gleeful anticipation of what you can and will accomplish. This is how self-assured people navigate the world: with a full tank of gas, with a GPS set to "success," with a confidence (okay, a swagger!) that is born out of realization that they've got what it takes to be exceptional.

WANT TO GO FOR IT?

Being authentic—being real—means accepting yourself for who you are. That comes from knowing and believing in your strengths. Where to start? The first thing you need to do is sit down with an insightful and loyal friend/and or colleague, and ask them to assess your best attributes. Ask them what makes you a standout and write it down. If they're confused about what you are looking for, give them a hint. Ask them, "What am I like when I'm dressed to the nines and looking terrific?" or "What would you consider my finest achievement?" or "How would you describe me if you had to be my reference for a new job?" Don't disagree with anything they say; just write it down.

After you thank your friend/colleague, construct her comments as a list, and tape that list to the inside of your medicine cabinet. Look at it every day, twice a day, whenever you brush your teeth. Now, memorize the qualities that make you feel most proud, say them aloud, and record them to your inner soundtrack. Every time you hear (in your head) a snide remark from an old sound loop, stop the machine and toss it out the window. Listen to me carefully: Only listen to the positive commentary that's flowing between your ears.

By the end of one month (okay, maybe two months), your playlist should be so energizing and exciting that you can walk to a meeting just listening to yourself, marveling at your capabilities. Think of the way you will command people's attention, the glamour you will project, the excitement you will incite, simply because you are listening to the inner voice confirming what you are capable of.

With this self-promoting loop playing softly in the background, you can tackle the business of your presentation—self-assured people have superb posture. Throw your shoulders back, hold your head up, and walk with purpose. Smile easily, to stranger and acquaintance alike. Be the first to greet, extending your hand to give a firm and warm handshake. Everything about your carriage underscores your confidence and verve: your curiosity and enthralled engagement with the world, an endless loop of affirmation and encouragement, a stunning presence marked by a confident demeanor, a happy and focused mindset that attracts equally positive and upbeat individuals into your life. What a package.

HERE'S WHAT YOU NEED TO DO:

To exude the confidence and panache that can only come from being authentically you:

1. **Look up the word "sprezzatura" and adopt it as your mantra.** Start each day with the premise that you're utterly terrific just the way you are. It doesn't matter if you're tall or short, fat, or thin, mousy haired or platinum blond—the genius of life is to plow ahead "full throttle" and not be afraid to experiment and even fail. As Woody Allen famously phrased it, "Eighty percent of success is showing up." While that may be true, it's the other twenty percent of complete and total engagement that will make you a star.

How to Take Yourself Out to Dinner

There comes a moment in every grown-up's life when he or she must dine alone. There is nothing to fear. Here's what to do:

- Select a restaurant with a decidedly unstuffy atmosphere. Consider a restaurant with a lively bar where you can eat right at the counter.
- No, Burger King, Taco Bell, and Friendly's do not count as restaurants.
- Make a reservation for 1.
- Now the most important thing: Select the reading material. What will it be? Something pretentious but unreadable like *The Nation*, something worldly and easy to flip through like *The New Yorker*, or a last-minute grab like *People* that won't raise any eyebrows but will keep you company throughout the meal?
- Take the phone but leave it in your pocket/purse. You're not expecting any calls and unless you're wearing scrubs, no one is going to think you're a brain surgeon.
- Even brain surgeons wear suits. (Who else can afford Brioni?)
- Arrive at the restaurant on time and review the table. If it's too close to the kitchen, refuse it on the spot.
- Look around the restaurant and make eye contact with total strangers. Hooray! You've just established your complete and total confidence.

2. **Fall in love with yourself.** Revel in your sharp wit, your marvelous ability to empathize, the ease with which you can throw a party. Whatever it is you're good at, make it your trademark. Listen to the soundtrack of reassuring affirmation and eliminate the noise of deriding messages. Take yourself out for dinner and delight in your company.

3. **Drop the mask and the guard (and the brick walls that keep you defensive and wary).** Open yourself up to others and don't be afraid of revealing who you are. Share your soul, your dreams, your doubts, your fears, and your joys with someone who's trustworthy and generous. Listen with empathy and unconditional acceptance when someone dares to share their hopes with you. These moments of true intimacy are all too rare. Savor them.

RESOURCES

I am absolutely wild for writers who show you how much fun it is to let it all hang out:

***Rare Bird of Fashion (The Irreverent Iris Apfel)* by Eric Boman**

Boman, Eric. *Rare Bird of Fashion (The Irreverent Iris Apfel).* New York: Thames & Hudson, Inc., 2007.

Fashion original and style maverick Iris Apfel admits she is "no great beauty," but she parlayed her extraordinary zest and originality into a look that's nothing short of genius. Her secret: She's real. She likes herself. She doesn't want to be anyone other than Iris Apfel.

Wacky Chicks: Life Lessons from Fearlessly Inappropriate and Fabulously Eccentric Women by Simon Doonan

Doonan, Simon. *Wacky Chicks: Life Lessons from Fearlessly Inappropriate and Fabulously Eccentric Women.*
New York: Simon & Schuster, 2003.

In Doonan's world, wacky chicks are women who are in charge of their own destinies, unencumbered by the need to conform, submit, or show insincere deference to what other people think or care about. In other words, they step out into the world convinced that they're already pretty fabu.

The Principles of Uncertainty by Maira Kalman

Of course. For more details, see the previous chapter.

3

Fabulous people are revered for their amazing attitude.

Attitude: The great decider of life. It doesn't really matter what we start out with—brains, beauty, charm, an excellent metabolism—our philosophy or worldview is the single best predictor of success. The reason: A great attitude is shorthand for "fun." Fun to be with, fun to eat with, fun to stand in line and wait for Dylan tickets with. Everyone wants to spend their time with life-affirming, positive people. And if professional success doesn't convince you, how about this: A great attitude is even more youth enhancing than Botox. It trumps wrinkles, creaky knees, and a tendency to repeat pointless anecdotes.

To those whose temperament leans to the negative, or God forbid, *dyspeptic,* the notion of a great attitude may seem overwhelmingly difficult. I will not lie; it takes a disciplined mind to reframe life's curveballs and body slams and still come out on top. But, once you do (and you will), you will wake up every morning with this unbeatable urge to wring every ounce of fun out of the day. Forgive me if I sound inspirational but in short, **attitude is everything.**

What the Fruit Man Taught Me

A few summers ago, I started asking Joseph Kankam, the young man that tended the fruit in my local organic supermarket, "When do you expect the Honeycrisp apples?" Joseph assured me the apples would be arriving in the fall.

In mid-September, I walked into the grocery and was greeted by Joseph's broad smile. "The apples have arrived," he said. "Would you like a taste?" Of course I said yes. Joseph went to get his paring knife and then we stood in the middle of the aisle and shared my first Honeycrisp apple of the season.

This story sums up everything I believe in:

- Happiness is contagious. The few moments in Joseph's company assured me a wonderful evening ahead. My mood was elevated and heightened for the rest of the week—I wanted to share the story of the apple with everyone I met.

- Likeability is a critical component to success. There are lots of smart, savvy people who undermine their own possibilities with a negative, brusque manner. Big mistake. We want to buy apples from people who make us feel good about ourselves.

- "Only connect." In *Howard's End*, E.M. Forster's characters struggle with the difficulties of creating ties. By remembering my enthusiasm for Honeycrisp apples, Joseph let me know how much he values our relationship. He converted me from a shopper to an admirer. And our relationship has stuck.

- Lead with passion. It doesn't matter what you do—trade stocks, run a bank, or repair dishwashers—your excitement and enthusiasm for your product, your company, and yourself is a critical component to success. Get up every morning believing you're selling the world's best apples.

- Take pride in what you do, for its own sake. I would wager that Joseph didn't get a commission on the five apples I bought that day.

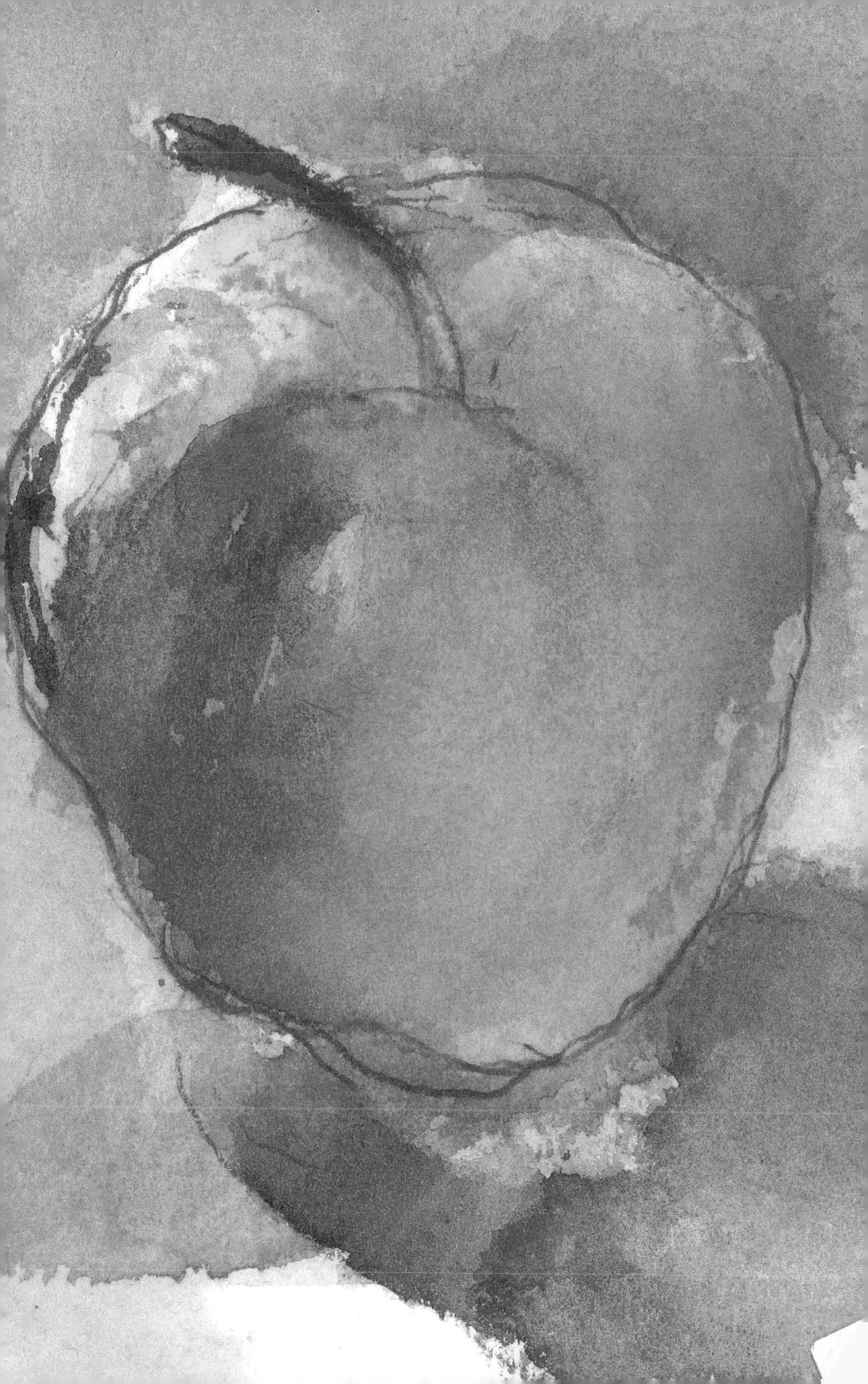

WHERE TO START:

How do fabulous people maintain that terrific attitude?

They are grateful for the small stuff.

I'm no evangelist but if you consider each day a gift, you're going to be awfully happy. Stop focusing on the "coulda/woulda" and just make every day a little brighter for yourself and others. (While you're at it, would you mind holding the door if you see me coming?)

They are fun to be with.

People who exude happiness are magnetic. We want to work with them, play with them, eat lunch with them. We're even willing to fetch their biryani rice from the salad bar if that's what it takes to be part of their lives. And why not? Happy people get things done. They look for opportunities to maximize their happiness. They whistle while they work so the day flies by. They refuse to cave to self-doubt. They want the fun of success (not just the success). And they want you to have fun too.

They are genius at reframing.

Rather than cave when things get tough, the happy and optimistic types go analytic, looking at the various options that keep their goals in sight. They know that life is only a straight road if you're afraid of taking a big plop! There will always be detours and roadblocks and potholes that can knock you off course—but these will not keep you from the final destination, if you have chosen to stay the course. And besides, these happy types adore a detour; after all, it

How Attitude Attracts Success

Positive people send out subtle and nonverbal "metamessages" that indicate high energy and full presence. These metamessages act as a centrifugal force, attracting opportunities, new acquaintances, and an aura of confidence and accomplishment. A marvelous attitude trumps everything, including aptitude. Optimistic or upbeat thinking isn't Pollyana-ish but a deliberate reframing of a negative situation.

How can you tell what kind of attitude you have?

- If you're prone to saying, "I'll never be able to do that" or "It's never going to work," you've got a bad attitude.
- On the other hand, if you say things like, "Is there anyone who knows how to do this?" or "Let's review what we've done in the past so we can see if there's a new approach that might work," you've got a good attitude.
- Superbly talented people with a bad attitude will be derailed sooner or later.
- Unless it's life threatening, most situations are fixable. Lighten up!
- A great attitude needs to be fed, watered, and/or petted, so jettison frenemies, archrivals, and jealous competitors from your galaxy.

may bring them somewhere even more interesting than the original destination.

People who are happy are incorrigibly hopeful. They're resilient and optimistic even in the face of daily disappointments. They believe in themselves and their capabilities. This is what steadies them when times are tough. They refuse to submit to defeatist thinking and behaviors. (You might wonder, *"Are they overly medicated?"* but you would be wrong.) When times get tough, instead of folding their tents, they start reframing. They look for options that will still get them to the goal, such as picking up the phone to schedule a chat with their brainiest of colleagues, or ordering in lunch for a creative session in the office. They refuse to believe all is lost when they know there are other ways to get to the destination. So why pack it all in?

They are pit-bullish, upbeat thinkers.

People who are happy are also disciplined. Just as they will not skip the morning ablutions no matter how miserable they feel, happy people will not tolerate a negative mindset. They know that a good attitude requires a kind of steely, disciplined pursuit of upbeat and optimistic thinking. They do not submit to the normal and irritating vicissitudes of life and disparage their own efforts. Oh, no. When everything goes grim and dark, they make their bed, pull their socks up (or order new white-on-white polka dot anklets from a chic boutique), get their car washed, and head back into the world with a great big smile, their energy and vitality on full display. Even if it's just for show, they will never ruin someone else's day with a surly, self-pitying state of mind.

And finally, there's the *cockeyed optimism* factor and its delicious impact on the world. I just can't live without cockeyed optimists. Their zany, crazy, delicious refusal to see anything but the goodness and greatness in every step and every misstep is terribly seductive. It's a wonder how they sleep at night with their forever-evolving theories and interpretations. But—and it's a big "but"—we need to push our cynicism aside and watch them very carefully. We must emulate their every move because these masters of the cockeyed, impossible-to-defeat, relentlessly optimistic universe are having a fabulous time of it (and we can too).

They know how and when to laugh it off.

When it comes to sense of humor, there are people who refuse to see the fun in any situation (and make everything painful and exhausting) and the people who see the fun in *every* situation (and are surrounded by devoted and admiring fans wherever they go).

That's what makes the fabulous utterly and completely *phenomenal!* While they take the important things in life (work, friends, relationships, feelings, the world!) seriously, they tend not to take *themselves* too seriously, so they can move about with ease and lightheartedness. They are not burdened by hubris. On the contrary. Their lives are too full, too rich with potential, to get bogged down by wasteful and doltish superciliousness.

They're also smart. They know that effectiveness is buttressed and amplified by a sense of satisfaction. In other words, nothing greases the wheels better than laughter.

Show Me the Brio

You would think that when interviewed about architect Frank Gehry, artists, colleagues, and clients would focus on his amazing gifts for sculptural forms. That they would wax rhapsodic about his phenomenal ability to bend materials so that they undulate like slivering snakes.

And they did. In filmmaker Sydney Pollack's documentary *Sketches by Frank Gehry,* Gehry was heralded as one of the greatest architects of this century. But what I found most fascinating was the emphasis on fun. Clients loved working with Gehry because he was fun. Artists mentioned Gehry's great sense of humor. And colleagues commented on his brio, which *Merriam-Webster's Dictionary* defines as "vigor and vivacity."

Show me the brio.

According to Daniel Goleman in his seminal book *Working with Emotional Intelligence*, "The greatest difference between average and superior leaders is in their emotional style. The most effective leaders are more outgoing, more emotionally expressive, more likable." To paraphrase screenwriter William Goldman, "The people who get work in Hollywood are more fun to be with." There's that word again . . . fun.

To demonstrate brio, one must discipline oneself to stay resilient and optimistic in the face of daily disappointments. To do that, we must become aware of what's going on inside our heads. Self-talk that's diminishing, deprecating, and demoralizing is going to limit our opportunities. Frank Gehry didn't get to be Frank Gehry by telling himself he was a rotten architect.

Brio takes confidence and energy. It requires humor. You need to be excited about what you do. You need a sense of purpose. And you must communicate that excitement through every form of communication, including image and actions.

For high-performers, it's not enough just to get the work done. They want something deeper, richer, more satisfying in their working relationships. They're in pursuit of the fun of success.

HOW DO YOU DO IT?

How do you dump the ballast from your boat and sail glee-fully to your destination?

1. **Let's start with the obvious: Lighten up!** Sure, life is filled with deprivations and disappointments and it's not easy to laugh as much as we should. But showing up for your appointment with LIFE and acting glum and mood disordered is terribly unattractive.

2. **Relax. Don't take yourself so seriously.** You're a lot more fun to be with when you're not lording over people with your inflated sense of importance.

3. **Make sure there's at least one person in your life who can turn the clock back and remind you how good it is to be a goof-off.** This is important, especially as you get older and your need for silliness and frivolity increases exponentially.

4. **Throw caution to the wind.** Every now and then do something that's really unexpected and at the same time good for your soul. Wear an absolutely drop dead black dress to work, with heels, for no other reason than you look and feel amazing in it. Buy a beret and say "bonjour" instead of "good morning." Sing out loud while riding a bicycle.

Whatever it takes to get you to feel the excitement about your life, do it.

Postscript: No matter how old you are, you've got to be obsessed by something and set some goals—racing a sports car, mastering a soufflé, planting a garden—and no matter what the obstacles, you've got to be determined to achieve those goals. Or get close to those goals. Or as close to those goals as you can get. Spend time with people who are always in the throes of some new passion, and breathe in that excitement. Let that big, overwhelming need to utilize every gift and talent at their disposal trigger something inside of you. Everything matters, especially when it has to do with discovering and fulfilling the purpose of your life.

Maybe it boils down to something as simple as this: Keep going. Never stop making lists—of things to do and the reasons that you're the only one who can do them. Keep reminding yourself of your intrinsic goodness and spend zero (zero!) time obsessing about all the things you're not. Get up in the morning determined to make the day fun and productive. And wear your most gorgeous clothes—save nothing! Looking good, thinking beautiful thoughts, and acting as if you were the most sensational creature on the planet is the most effective way to mastermind the narrative of your life.

RESOURCES

When I get lost in the thicket of insecurity and need to reclaim my mojo, I read:

***Eccentric Glamour: Creating an Insanely More Fabulous You* by Simon Doonan**

Doonan, Simon. *Eccentric Glamour: Creating an Insanely More Fabulous You.* New York: Simon & Schuster Paperbacks, 2008.

By interviewing some of the world's most intriguing and, shall we say, *original* people, Doonan makes the case that attitude (an unbeatable combination of charisma, charm, and personal energy) is what makes them simply irresistible.

On Becoming a Leader by Warren Bennis

Bennis, Warren. *On Becoming a Leader.*
Reading, MA: Addison-Wesley Publishing Company, Inc., 1989.

In trying to define what it is to be a leader, Bennis also examines the role of attitude in success, arguing that childlike enthusiasm and an open mind may be more important than the cachet of a graduate school degree.

The Big Sister's Guide to Work: The Inside Rules Every Working Girl Must Know by Marcelle DiFalco and Jocelyn Greenky Herz

DiFalco, Marcelle, and Jocelyn Greenky Herz. *The Big Sister's Guide to Work: The Inside Rules Every Working Girl Must Know.*
New York: Fireside, 2005.

A clever, witty, and informative all-you-need-to-know-to-get-ahead-in-life manifesto, with an emphasis on brushing up on the habits that can finesse your trajectory (stay late, come in early, say hello, and always have something nice to say about your boss behind his/her back).

4

Fabulous people are warm and completely accessible.

In a world that slobbers over über cool, let me make the pitch for something equally seductive: über warmth. There is nothing more compelling or persuasive than speaking with someone who is interested in you, someone who honors even an impromptu visit with rapt attention. I've had it with the multitaskers who stare at the screen instead of searching my face for clues; I am *so over* the tense beauties with their stony and inscrutable stares. You wanna know what's truly fabulous? Someone who knows how to establish a rapport, tries to understand me, and most importantly, encourages me to feel good about myself when we're together. As Eliza Doolittle put it, "Don't talk of love; show me!"

WHERE TO START:

I shall have to make a confession here:

I love the grand gesture, the air of *gemütlichkeit.* Please . . . enough with the frosty Eskimo types who make me go *brrrr* when I'm in their presence. This alluring quality, warmth, is so easy to master that everyone (well, almost everyone) can

Just try to resist a smile. I-m-p-o-s-s-i-b-l-e.

do it. It happens the moment you start communicating and it can be whittled down to its essence: expressiveness, gifted listening, and a desire (no, make that *thirst!*) for true connectedness. Think about it . . . the smile, the eye contact, the way someone's body responds to what you're saying. The ease in which they greet you, the way they listen so ardently, so intent on understanding what you have to say. You feel heard, which is indeed priceless, and very much in sync.

I've heard all the rationales and (frankly lame) explanations for why this doesn't happen more frequently. The *I'm so busy* factor: We're so busy trying to get everything done that we don't have the time to be courteous and gracious. The *I'm so overextended* factor: If I make eye contact, I might have to engage with someone and then lose my precious momentum.

The *I don't want to lose my focus* factor: My life is simply too important to throw away on an encounter that could be, but might not be, authentically rich and meaningful.

If you're as fed up as I am with the shallow and insincere encounters that masquerade as "relationships," here's what you need to know:

A warm and convivial encounter is memorable.

When you're around someone who's sociable, someone with his light on, it's like a shot in the arm. Nope, sorry, it's more akin to an infusion of oxygen going straight into the main artery. So why don't we do it more often?

Life really is unfair. We're so tethered to technology that we're depriving ourselves of a good laugh and maybe, if we're awfully lucky, a hug. If you get the opportunity to meet with someone, put it out there. Blast them with your openhearted and generous way of being. Come armed with a clever anecdote or a witty and self-deprecating story that will get the ball rolling. Search for clues (the eyes, the complexion, the posture) that might indicate someone who can use a pair of shoulders to lean on. A small moment of honesty (and a little mirth) might be the brightest moment in someone's day.

Warmth is typified by facial expressions that indicate genuine interest.

Warmth comes from your smile, your easy laugh, the way your face reflects and responds to the conversation. Don't sleepwalk through your life with a vacant stare and then wail about loneliness. Do something gutsy and proven to work: Get rid of that "don't bother me" expression that keeps everyone away and replace it with a twinkle that's both impish and flirtatious. Best part about it? Those without a pulse won't dare look you in the eye. (Forgive me, but do you really need another zombie in your life?)

Warmth is listening—giving someone your full and undivided attention when they're speaking.

I know, I know, it's tough to stay interested when you're not surrounded by Cole Porter-type raconteurs, but please, be patient. Don't over-talk, interrupt, or jump to get a word in edgewise, and will ya knock it off on the one-up responses? (We get it: You always fly first class.) Just listen to what we're

How to Talk About Yourself Without Putting People into a Coma

- Don't even think about talking about your latest exploits before ascertaining the good health and sanity of the person you're speaking with.
- Inquire as to how they're doing. Listen closely. Ask interested and relevant follow-up questions.
- When it's your turn to talk about yourself, make sure the other person is listening. If he's not listening, cut to the chase and very pleasantly say, "Everything's good."
- However, if the person is sincerely interested, they'll appreciate authentic responses.
- Don't boast, don't brag, don't go on and on, but for God's sake, don't diminish or play down your latest exploit. If it was good, say it! (Talk about what you're doing in a way that gets the listener to feel included. Don't say, "We're traveling out of the country," when you could say, "We're taking a cruise to Portofino.")
- Don't be intentionally oblique. "Did I tell you that I've gotten the go-ahead on the thing I was working on? I think it's going to be very good" is so lame. Be specific. Spill. Share the details. Turn your anecdote into a story that's fun to listen to. Don't dilute your enthusiasm. (Trust me; it's exciting to be around someone who's committed to what they are doing.)
- Avoid name-dropping unless it's intrinsic to your story. Even then, do we really need to know that some B-list celebrity ate at the same joint you did?
- Maintain eye contact throughout the conversation to accurately gauge whether the listener has slipped into a conversation-induced coma.

How to Show Warmth When Your Basal Temperature Runs Cold

- Redefine and view warmth as a clever and strategic edge and not as a pushover without a spine.
- Master The Hug. It's all about a friendly, simpatico hold that brilliantly conveys a feeling of sympathy and admiration, and allows a connection rather than a seduction. (The Obamas are geniuses at The Hug.)
- Practice smiling. Practice, practice, practice so it becomes your default facial expression.
- Try not to think about you all of the time. I know it's tough, especially when you find your life so mesmerizing, but you need to think about me *in a cozy kind of way* when we're interacting.
- Put all toys away when we're face-to-face.
- Do something extraordinary when there's an opportunity. Your neighbor's son has impeccable manners? Write her a note and let her know.
- Cross the street and initiate a chat when you see an acquaintance, rather than just wave. (*Ay caramba!* That dismissive wave!)
- Don't skimp on the compliments. Notice everything, from a new haircut to the genius decision to wear plum colored socks with purple patent loafers.
- Never send a prewritten thank-you note, a rubber-stamped holiday greeting, or a text-messaged sympathy note from a BlackBerry or iPhone. (*Yikes*, people!)
- Think you're scared? That guy at the cocktail party is shaking like a leaf. Go over and invite him to join your little group.

saying (and listen for what we might not be saying, too) so the engagement feels genuine and touches our souls.

Warmth is looking people straight in the eye when speaking.

Search their face for clues to their inner mood state. If you sense a problem and have the time, use your sympathetic listening skills (a face that mirrors the pain) to let them know that you would be honored to help.

Warmth is always "rapport talk," rather than "report talk."

In her seminal book, *You Just Don't Understand: Women and Men in Conversation,* linguist Deborah Tannen distinguishes between the kind of talk that focuses on personal experience and builds alliances (a.k.a. "rapport talk") with the kind of conversation that centers on the exchanging of information ("report talk"). Now, do I really need to tell you that rapport talk is a big, fat blast of good fun? And by the way, while women tend to be more adept at rapport talk, there are also exceptions. There are certain women who would rather discuss chicken than feelings and certain men who can establish intimacy through willful philosophizing on sneaker versus chukka boot. To really connect, you must not retreat into any conversation that seems canned and hackneyed, predictable or formulaic—or involves fowl.

HOW TO DO IT:

To exude that gentle heat that can instantly defrost even the well defended, you might:

1. **Force yourself to slow down.** It doesn't matter what industry or profession you're in; it's still all about relationships and how you connect, one to one.

2. **Pay attention.** When getting together for a meeting or an impromptu chat, make it meaningful by eschewing the hi-tech toys for the warm-touch experience.

3. **React, respond, and relate to what you're hearing.** Don't be afraid to show that you're moved by an admission of fear or pain . . . consider it an honor that someone would trust you with their troubles.

RESOURCES

When your heat-seeking missile needs a tune-up, curl up and read:

Emotional Intelligence: Why It Can Matter More Than IQ
by Daniel Goleman

Goleman, Daniel. *Emotional Intelligence: Why It Can Matter More Than IQ.* United States: Bantam, 1995.

Goleman's theories on why people succeed in life revolutionized the way we looked at "smart." Instead of judging people on their test-taking prowess, Goleman looks at how our ability to connect and form intimate relationships (just one aspect of "emotional intelligence") can play a much more powerful role in predicting long-term success.

Do One Nice Thing: Little Things You Can Do to Make the World a Lot Nicer by Debbie Tenzer

Tenzer, Debbie. *Do One Nice Thing: Little Things You Can Do to Make the World a Lot Nicer.*
New York: Crown Publishers, 2009.

Tenzer got fed up listening to self-centered commentary and decided to do something about the rampant selfishness we take for granted. Her stroke of genius was to see all the warm and wonderful things we can do to make the world a happier place. Her recommendations range from encouraging your kids to say hello to strangers, and flooding a sick friend with visits and cards, to offering to write a personal recommendation for someone just in case they need it down the line.

How to Win Friends and Influence People by Dale Carnegie

Carnegie, Dale. *How to Win Friends and Influence People.*
New York: Pocket Books, 1936.

Back in the old days, before Oprah and Dr. Phil, there was Dale Carnegie blazing the trail of persuasion and influence, the key ingredients to a charismatic presence. Carnegie's discovery: There is a method to get people to like you. The six critical steps to likeability include: 1.) Be genuinely interested in other people. 2.) Smile. 3.) Remember a person's name. 4.) Encourage others to talk about themselves. 5.) Find the link to a person's interests. 6.) Make the other person feel important.

Fabulous people have flair.

5

A young friend sends word of a marvelous "spotting." She was sitting at a bar in Georgetown and saw Rahm Emanuel, White House chief of staff at the time, holding court in white jeans and a navy velvet blazer. "Ellen, you would have died," she swoons most appropriately, as what could be more fabulous than putting stuffy Washington on notice that there's a new game in town?

There are those who inherit flair from a fabled grandmother along with the pearls, and then there are those who figure it out by themselves by observing and experimenting, making their personal presentation into a brilliant extension of how they look at the world. A person with flair has the remarkable combination of style and self, a brainy desire to stand out and be noticed right from the beginning (with a good-humored nod and wink).

It's probably written in the Bible, for God's sake:
Every human being needs a crisp, white shirt.

Style is shorthand, a visual clue to your authority and confidence. By selecting and wearing the clothes and accessories that illuminate your individuality, you telegraph to the world that your good opinion matters. And lest anyone think flair connotes vapid self-absorption, let's set the record straight: Flair takes years of observation, thinking, experimentation, and practice until you get the details just right.

Unlike the fashion slaves who live in fear of making a mistake, the stylish are only concerned with two things: finding the elegant solution to looking good, no matter their age or size, and maximizing their fun in everyday life.

If you're properly intrigued with the idea of boosting your flair/style quotient, may I suggest we consider these elements of style from the fabulous ones . . .

WHERE TO START:

They wear clothes that add oomph not ouch.

Go to your closet and separate your clothes according to two mood states: Happy and Sad.

The clothes that are itchy, ill fitting, uncomfortable, too small, too tight, too narrow, too wide, too unflattering, too-too-too depressing must be banished from your closet. You cannot expect to wear mood-disorder-causing clothes with any jocularity or wit.

On the other hand, the clothes that make you look and feel gorgeous, the clothes that you want to touch and stroke because they are so beautiful, the clothes that make you look leaner, longer, more original and intriguing, the clothes that keep your spirits airborne no matter how long a day you're going to have—those are the clothes that you keep because they will serve as the foundation to your personal style.

They do not worship labels.

That is not to say the truly stylish do not appreciate fine clothes and impeccable tailoring. *Au contraire.* But the fabulous do not fill their closet with clothes that were purchased because of the price or because they appeared in a magazine. When the fabulous do buy something, it's because it fits perfectly (or can be altered), it makes them feel terrific, and hopefully it will help them maintain the memorable and intriguing image they're always working on. And those over-the-top pieces that can keep you up at night? Well, everyone is entitled to at least two *coup de foudre* moments in their lifetime, because it will make them deliriously happy.

Clothes have transformational power. They can summon up a memory. They can wipe away the years. Hell, a fabulous pantsuit with a starchy white shirt can even wipe away the tears. Remember: Clothes tell the story of how you see yourself.

Clothes should be armor—tough enough to wear on a six-hour flight but somehow able to get you to your destination looking chic. Clothes should give you the confidence to say hello to total strangers because you're positive they will want to make your acquaintance. Clothes that you love and love you back will never go out of style or fashion . . . they are immune to trends and whimsies.

In my head I've already written a book titled *The Clothes I Have Loved* and my love affair with:

Black pants. Can you ever have enough black pants? Ah, but you must have a pair of sleek and tailored black pants that lift the glutes and de-emphasize the hips and are worn long enough to cover the front of the shoe. These pants should have loops for a belt so you can wear them with a wardrobe of sharply tailored shirts, Bohemian-inspired fitted turtlenecks, or with a fitted white shirt that's worn over the waistline (with the last button unbuttoned).

Grey cardigan. You do not need a cardigan in purple, eggplant, citrine, or sand. You must have a grey cardigan in your closet. It will look good buttoned. It will look good unbuttoned. And it will look sensational thrown over your shoulders when the air gets nippy, or tied around your waist when you've had a bacchanal type of weekend.

Simple, white cotton shirt. I would love to write a sonnet to the white shirt. It is ol' dependable. It will make you look younger, fresher, energized. It will connote authority, competence, and cool-headed *savoir faire*. You can wear it in the evening with a black *peau de soie* skirt and in the morning with a slim-fit pair of slacks (and of course the grey cardigan). And on the weekends when everyone else is deluding themselves into thinking no one is looking at them and wearing their most frumpy and unattractive "weekend garb," you will be noticed with admiration for the way you put together a pair of great jeans, a white shirt, a gutsy belt, and beat-up white sneakers.

A safari-style jacket in olive drab. It may take you a lifetime to find it, but you need a jacket in olive drab that's not too short and not too long, but just right. You will wear this jacket a million times and never grow bored with its simplicity and verve. You will wear it with a pencil skirt and a crisp white shirt (and the highest of heels!) and you will wear it with a pair of grey flannel pants or chinos, a grey wool crewneck sweater, and a pair of lovingly maintained cordovan loafers. And when everyone else is wearing this year's cape or wrap or jacket of the moment, you will go to your closet and pull out the safari jacket and look sharper than anybody else.

Trouser-inspired jeans. I'll admit it: I was late to this party. I didn't get it at first how utterly stunning you can look in a pair of jeans that are tailored like trousers (belt loops, pockets, dark denim or black rinse) worn with a crisp white shirt, a fitted blazer (navy or graphite grey), and a pair of tiny-heeled loafers or brogues. But I get it now. Every one should have a pair of knockout jeans in the closet.

A classic raincoat. Remember that final scene in *Breakfast at Tiffany's* when Holly Golightly (Audrey Hepburn) is standing in the rain wearing the most perfect (and simple) raincoat? That's the coat to look for.

They wear the same clothes over and over again.

If you have flair and therefore an original point of view, you are freed of the concerns and the constraints of worrying (needlessly) about what people might think of you. And you will certainly be freed of the concerns and constraints about wearing the same clothes over and over again.

A story:

I shared an office (in one of New York City's Gothic-style buildings with casement windows that actually opened . . . I get misty-eyed just thinking about it) with a woman of great charm. She was a senior executive with a fashion public relations firm, and I was a lowly and part-time freelancer. Every Monday the woman wore a pair of sharply tailored, black

Introduction to Under-the-Radar Dressing 101

- The late fashion meteor Tina Chow wore Hanes white tee-shirts (three to a pack) with an YSL pantsuit.

- Uniqlo (www.uniqlo.com) is Japan's answer to The Gap except they've asked über-designer Jil Sander, famed for her excruciatingly simple and purist look, to create a $100-and-less collection for them. *Not to be believed.*

- Target got on the warpath early with its relationship with iconoclastic designer Isaac Mizrahi. Today it's the place to find racer-back maxi tee-shirt dresses by Massimo for under $30.

- Nothing looks older than piling on the "important" jewelry. Go to www.oneworldprojects.com and buy the recycled plastic bracelets from Burkina Faso ($3.50 each). Buy at least five. Some might call it socially responsible—I call it pure genius.

- Wouldn't dream of shopping at Payless Shoes? You're crazy . . . they're knocking off the Louboutins and the Blahniks left foot and right foot.

- Always wear accessories in odd numbers—three strands of tagua nuts, five African recycled plastic bracelets, a stack of wedding bands.

- American Apparel seems to have nailed the leggings look and they're affordably priced. Buy a pair in black and wear with a long A-line skirt and a small, fitted top. For the shoes, either a pair of clunky black oxfords or black ballerinas.

- Don't be afraid to either tart up (tight jeans with a peep-toe clog) or mumsy (a little sweater set, perhaps?) a look. Instead of counting sheep, shop the closet.

- Zappos.com for sneakers by Superga. Trust me.

- I'm sorry but a pretentious logo-ed wallet in a pretentious logo-ed handbag? Have some self-respect.

wool, wide-legged French sailor trousers with a black turtleneck. Every Wednesday, she wore the same black trousers with an ecru turtleneck. And on Friday, she wore the black trousers with a crisp white shirt. A plain black leather belt with an understated buckle and a pair of polished black flat loafers completed the look. Forgive me; I do not remember what she wore on Tuesday and Thursday, because it doesn't matter. What matters is that she wore the black trousers three days a week. And didn't apologize for it. In fact, we discussed her wardrobe one time over coffee and she made it quite clear that she was a firm believer in, "Buy the best that you can afford and wear it over and over again."

I do not need to tell you that this stunning woman was oozing with flair. Every detail was first-rate. Her pants fit her perfectly, her turtleneck sweaters were of fine cashmere. And her white shirt was tailored and in immaculate condition. There was nothing superfluous in what she wore . . . it was style at its zenith.

They swear by the basics but the basics are perfect.

Can you believe there are still women roaming the earth who wear themselves out shopping, afraid to repeat what they wore the week before, or even the day before? What a bore.

The truly stylish create a wardrobe composed of a small number of superb pieces that can be worn in a myriad of ways. The wardrobe is made up of classic pieces—black and/or grey trousers, trouser-like jeans, white shirts, black boots, black pumps and/or loafers, a pencil skirt, a black turtleneck, and a coat that telegraphs wit and verve. And then they punch it up . . . buying vintage, costume, and classic jewelry, amusing

The Shine Does Cost Extra. (Time, That Is.)

- Your friends may "act" shocked when you admit to needing two hours to get ready in the morning but, trust me, they notice.
- Oxy-Clean, Zout, Seventh Generation, and a dry cleaner familiar with cleaning difficult and challenging fabrics must be a part of your life.
- Shoes should be shined regularly—at least every third wearing.
- In a Ziploc bag put together a shoe maintenance kit that includes rubber gloves, an old rag (men's undershirts are perfect), Meltonian shoe polish in the standard black/brown/cordovan/neutral, and a stiff brush for removing "schmutz" from a rainstorm. Keep this kit under the bathroom sink and shine your shoes while you're waiting for the glycolic mask or exfoliating pad to do its work.
- All fine shoes deserve wooden shoe trees to maintain their shape. If you're feeling a pinch, first spray the inside of the shoe with Kiwi Shoe Stretch Spray and then insert the shoe trees. Leave overnight. Miracle in a can!
- Did you know that interviewers make snap decisions about your capabilities based upon the condition of your shoes? In addition to a gleaming shine, that includes fresh heels and toe caps that are smooth.
- Brooks Brothers makes a "no-iron" shirt that's nothing short of amazing. Remove shirts from the dryer after 25 minutes and place on a wire hanger. (Buy shirts on sale.)
- Before putting clothes back into the closet, examine under a harsh light and look for telltale signs of coffee stains, salad dressing "flicks," and ballpoint pen marks on your cuff.
- Never use a rotating "de-piller" on fine sweaters. Instead, gently snip off pills with a cuticle scissor.

hats, a purse that's practical yet elegant, a jaunty scarf, an umbrella in a subversively happy color. They juxtapose the solemnity of classic attire with the frivolity of imaginative accessories.

Believe me, no one will question the authority of wearing a look of this intelligence and elegance over and over again.

They are obsessed with accessories.

Flair is your imprint, your personal mark of originality. It has nothing to do with fashion . . . we're talking timeless here. And let's not forget the insouciant factor, for someone with flair is always slightly subversive, trying to wring pleasure out of the predictable or formulaic.

Finding accessories that help you create an intriguing look requires opening your eyes to the world around you. You must find your inspiration from the people around you and then develop the requisite fearlessness that enables you to stop someone on the street, compliment their marvelous ensemble, and ask if they can direct you to where it was purchased.

Flair is jettisoning fixed ideas of who you are and how you are supposed to look, and then going full speed ahead . . . and never looking back when you find yourself in a junk shop and panting over a necklace of faux pearls the size of robin's eggs.

Flair is giving good taste the boot . . . or at least an ankle boot . . . if you're convinced that this slightly trashy looking jacket will rev up the perfectly ladylike pencil skirt that you've always worn with a perfectly respectable sweater.

Stylish Shoppers' Secret Tips

- Go alone, so if you want to splurge you don't feel compelled to explain.
- Why/who would you have to explain to anyway? (Are you still getting an allowance?)
- Don't go when you're cranky or irritable. I'm no fan of retail therapy.
- Look glamorous. Salespeople will take you a lot more seriously.
- The night before you shop, make a list of all the things you own (and love) so you're up to date on what you have. Tuck that list inside your wallet. Refer to it when you're about to cave to another black turtleneck.
- Only work with a salesperson who is oozing charm and *joie de vivre* (and looks pretty fabulous herself).
- The salesperson is wrong when he/she insists the wool pants in aubergine will be a fabulous addition to your closet. No one needs aubergine pants.
- You will rue the day you bought the too-small pants, thinking you'd diet your way into them.
- Bring a bottle of water, a Listerine PocketPak, and deftly reapply the lipstick throughout the shopping to shore up your flagging energies.
- Don't buy anything in stores that are "store credit only."
- On your way in or out, make a detour to the sock department. An extraordinary wardrobe always includes textured knee socks in black/brown, anklets to wear with Mary Janes, and a pair of mannish knee socks to wear with your most mummsiest of skirts (with high-heeled oxfords, of course).

Flair is winking at the mirror . . . having fun as you redefine and maybe even reinvent yourself so that your look is a perfect reflection of your creative energies and imagination.

Flair is always reveling in your too-muchness. Do not be chastened by the idea of standing out. Do not be afraid of wearing polka dots with stripes. It's your right, it's your privilege, it's your destiny. Do it!

HOW TO DO IT:

To create a singular image with the emphasis on flair/style rather than mindless fashion aping:

1. **Loosen up.** You know how you want to look. Stop pretending you're content wearing elasticized waist pants and lumpy sweaters when you'd really love to see yourself in a pair of gorgeous, high-waisted palazzo pants, a sharply tailored white blouse, and masses of faux amber beads. Hey kiddo, your life is not the dress rehearsal. Go find the costume that befits your dreams and wear it with exuberance.
2. **Recognize that style has nothing to do with body weight.** You may be larger than a stick insect or so petite you can't ride Disney World's "Space Mountain" but that does not mean you can't effect enormous panache. Find a shop that carries your size and see if they are grooving on the idea of creating an indelible look. Only work with a salesperson who is committed to helping you build a to-die-for wardrobe.
3. **Grow older and get wackier.** I mean it. Let's not get old; let's get crazier. Let's try things that once intimidated us . . . bolder accessories, stronger and more saturated

colors, vintage pieces from the resale shops, and white tee-shirts that come three to a pack like style icon Tina Chow wore. Let's not go gently into that good night . . . let's go screaming and fighting but looking awfully *smart* in our military jacket worn with a pair of matte black leggings.

RESOURCES

The minute I find myself eyeing elasticized waist pants, I drop everything and read:

***The Way We Lived Then: Recollections of a Well-Known Name Dropper* by Dominick Dunne**

Dunne, Dominick. *The Way We Lived Then: Recollections of a Well-Known Name Dropper.*
New York: Crown Publishers, 1999.

Flair is not just the way you present yourself—it's an attitude about the way you live your life. Dunne, a Hollywood insider who later became a first-rate journalist at *Vanity Fair* magazine, kept leather-bound notebooks filled with photographs and memorabilia about a time in Hollywood when its most rarefied inhabitants created magic off camera as well as on. From Sunday lunches in Malibu to candle-lit dinners in Bel Air, Dunne's group of friends knew the meaning of tireless party giving.

The One Hundred: A Guide to the Pieces Every Stylish Woman Must Own by Nina Garcia

Garcia, Nina. *The One Hundred: A Guide to the Pieces Every Stylish Woman Must Own.*
New York: HarperCollins Publishers, 2008.

If you've ever wondered why some people always look terrific, you need this book. Garcia has created the ultimate checklist of what you need in order to create a timeless and elegant wardrobe. A kinda Girl Scouts manual to looking *beyond amazing,* Garcia showcases the shoes, the shirts, the accessories that are serenely and confidently indifferent to trends.

The Barefoot Contessa Cookbook by Ina Garten

Garten, Ina. *The Barefoot Contessa Cookbook.*
New York: Clarkson Potter/Publisher, 1999.

I find Garten's tableware and serving accessories even more exciting than her recipes. I love the way she mixes the inexpensive platter with the ultra *haute* soup tureen . . . she approaches her table the same way a great dresser approaches her closet: Mix it up! Have fun! And always be true to your own point of view.

The truly fabulous have impeccable manners.

It's the scourge of modern life—the way we all have to accommodate ourselves to bad manners. You're familiar of course with all the *less-than-charming* moments that take place day after day and set our teeth on edge: not calling ahead to say you're running behind schedule. Taking a phone call while in the middle of a serious conversation. And even more glaringly *louche*, choosing not to send a handwritten thank-you note when someone has—like what?—written for you a personal recommendation or set up a job interview? Is it the multitasking or is something more ominous taking place?

Here's what I think: The people who are always looking for opportunities to be gracious and considerate are going to be liked, admired, loved, sought after, trusted, and have more access to palatial guest rooms in summer beach houses. And they will sleep better at night knowing that by making manners matter they really are at the top of their game.

Mr. W. Francis McGillicuddy
On the Pond
Water Mill, NY
11962

WHERE TO START:

Once you start living a life that's dictated by imaginative good sense, charm, and manners, the world is your oyster. But there are commandments that must be followed, and follow them we must:

Commandment 1.

Thou shalt show up, joyfully expectant.

If you're anywhere but the privacy of your boudoir, please bring with you your good cheer, interest in others, and unvarnished enthusiasm for life. Do not leave your personality on your hard drive.

Commandment 2.

Thou shalt show up, on time!

When everyone is trying to stuff their day and cram everything in, arriving on time is not just a godsend but a concrete measure of how much you respect and value my time. And if you're running behind schedule, for goodness' sake, call me and let me know so I have the option of doing something I need to do.

Commandment 3.

Thou shalt show no signs of boredom.

Look, everyone doesn't have your wit, your flair, and your prodigious memory for names, titles, obscure facts, or fabulous stories that keep everyone riveted in suspense. When in the presence of a less-than-scintillating mortal, try to be

A handwritten note that arrives in the mail is *a gift.*

sympathetic and absolutely never show boredom. Supercilious behavior is extraordinarily funny when viewed on Thursday night (*The Office*, anyone?), but it's most irritating and embarrassing when seen ringside.

Commandment 4.
Thou shalt initiate a greeting with eye contact and a warm handshake.

I can't imagine a simpler way to differentiate yourself from the 40-watt types who think it's perfectly acceptable to greet someone with a downcast look and a weak offer of a hand. There is a proper way to extend greetings to people and it's this easy: First, establish eye contact. Now extend your hand and take theirs, so that your hands are clasped together, web to web. Match the pressure of their hand until you're sure of the color of their eyes. Know the color? Go ahead; drop the hand. Think of a great handshake as the opening line to a movie: It sets up the plot and establishes character.

Commandment 5.
Thou shalt recognize that it's not (always) about you.

Hey, I'm the first one to say it's a good thing to like yourself, to enjoy your own company, and to toot your own horn. But people, come on: **It's. Not. (Always.) About. You.** Please control the impulse to commandeer every encounter by ruminating about your plans, your problems, and your achievements. Please refrain from playing "I'm Up/You're Down," the terribly off-putting habit of waiting for the moment to pounce and show someone up, when just listening and being happy for someone else is what we ought to do. Listen, I really am interested in you, but we also need to talk about *me* too if we're going to have a relationship.

Commandment 6.

Thou shalt revel in being old-fashioned.

Awright, I admit it: I'm a sucker for old-fashioned. I love black licorice buttons (R.I.P. Heide candies), cotton hankies, Bakelite flatware, and people who rise when offering their hand. And while we're on the subject of standing, I think it's sublimely genteel when a man or a woman gets up from his or her seat when I enter a room for the very first time.

And what about making sure you speak to the person on your right and your left when at a dinner table? Or waiting till everyone is served before digging in? Or sending a thank-you note to the host and hostess after a party? Little details . . . little details that pack such a punch!

Commandment 7.

Thou shalt maintain eye contact when conversing.

"Am I boring you?" That's what we're thinking when we see your eyes sweep the room while we're speaking to you. You do not have to speak to someone for the entire night but you must always show good manners and give someone your full attention when you're in a face-to-face encounter.

Commandment 8.

Thou shalt recognize that not everyone is plugged in.

Despite the ubiquity of smartphones, there are plenty of smart people who are not tethered to their e-mail for last-minute changes in appointments. It would make sense and be a lot more considerate to pick up a phone and call if a change has to be made. That excuse, "Oh, I sent you an e-mail," not only doesn't work but it brands *you* as a colossal idiot.

Commandment 9.
Thou shalt opt for meaningful introductions.

One of the pleasures in life is introducing someone with panache. Simply saying "Mary, this is Mike" is not going to create that recognition moment when two people realize they have something in common. That's where you come in.

A brilliant introduction is steeped in information about the two people you are introducing and a confidence that they will enjoy getting to know one another. Tell Mary something about Mike that she will find interesting. "Mary, Mike just moved from Lake Forest to run the account side for a big advertising firm. Didn't you live in Chicago a few years ago?" And then tell Mike something about Mary. "Mary is one of our company's top brand marketers and also races a vintage Porsche. Mike, you drive a Porsche, don't you?" Now step back and enjoy your handiwork. You've done it all—lauded their work, found the geographical connection, blessed the introduction with your *bonhomie.* Even if the conversation doesn't last, the impression *you'll* make will be indelible.

Commandment 10.
Thou shalt listen brilliantly.

Brilliant listening does not mean just keeping quiet when someone else is speaking—especially if you're just going to pick up where you left off when they finish. Oh, no. Brilliant listening is listening to what someone is saying (and what they're not saying) and asking those questions that get the conversation in high gear. Brilliant listening is 150-watt alertness, turning your body towards the speaker, and making them feel like they're witty, insightful, original, and oh so clever. Brilliant listening is looking for the moment to connect, to conspire, to turn an acquaintance into a friend,

Manners for the Etiquette-Challenged

- People who write handwritten thank-you notes after a dinner party are never forgotten.
- Maybe I'm a dinosaur but I still love it when a man steps back and allows the ladies to leave the elevator first.
- Both men and women can initiate a handshake.
- Look someone in the eye before extending your hand.
- Handshakes require web-to-web contact and must be held for as long as it takes to ascertain the color of the other person's eyes.
- Grip the person's hand with gusto but do not break any small bones.
- After the handshake is over, continue making eye contact.
- When placing a food order, it is not acceptable to simultaneously carry on a cellular conversation. Not even in the drive-thru.
- The minute you sit down at the table, place your napkin on your lap.
- The Good Lord created knives so that you wouldn't use your fingers to push food onto your fork.

and most importantly, to let them know your heart is open if the conversation needs to turn more personal.

Commandment 11.
Thou shalt seek a life of rich connectedness.

The world is lonely. It's hard to find love and friendship. People are "bowling alone." So why are we going out of our way to disconnect? We're all guilty. We abbreviate a phone call with call waiting. We say we need to take the cell phone call when we *don't.* We stand in line waiting for our low-fat latte and instead of drumming up a conversation with our line-mates, we play games, read e-mail, or update our Facebook status to say we're standing in line waiting for our low-fat latte. We don't pay enough attention so we conveniently ignore the barista's telltale puffy eyes or hand's tremble. We travel in a bubble of blithe disconnectedness—saddened and maddened by the hi-tech-ness and the lack of warm touch-ness.

Face it, folks, there are fewer and fewer opportunities to be fabulous in a world gone virtual (and clueless). Will you please grab every one of them?

Get up in the morning and extend yourself. Say hello to everyone you meet—the guys in the elevator, the parking lot attendant, everyone! When the phone rings, answer it with a smile on your face and state your name so that the caller knows they've hit the jackpot: Someone on their game! Socialize with lots of different people, oozing enthusiasm. Pay attention to the people around you and let them know you're emotionally present and accessible. Look gorgeous every day so that you're always ready to meet someone new . . . someone who might change your life, enhance your work, or, at the least, make you feel wonderful about being you. Take pride in your work! Whatever you do, give it everything you've got so that you're creating a reputation for excellence. Leave nothing to chance.

To underscore that you're a living, breathing, incredibly thoughtful, and oh-so-considerate human being:

1. **Consider your manners** as if they were an over-the-top, filled-to-the-brim, veritable jewel box of vintage and crisply modern accessories ready to be worn for any occasion. There are times when affecting an old-fashioned sense of decorum is essential and other times when you need to finesse the subtleties of contemporary life.

2. **Go out of your way to show respect to everyone.** Ever hear of the phrase *noblesse oblige*? Look it up and try it on for size. It's not only nice—it has the added effect of making you look like an *über mensch.*

3. **Try to be unconditionally accepting to those you care about.** It's not easy just to sit back and say very little, but it will encourage honesty and authenticity.

WANT TO GO FOR IT?

What effortless poise and a command of good manners will get you:

- **Charisma.** The centrifugal force that just moves more and more interesting, intriguing, and like-minded (i.e., caring, considerable, well-mannered) people into your orbit. Who wouldn't want a few more sensitive souls at their Fourth of July BBQ?

- **An enviable reputation.** Whether it precedes your entrance or follows you like a puppy, you must cultivate a reputation for beautiful gestures, extraordinary thoughtfulness, and a gift for making people feel good in your presence.

- **Stealth (but real) power.** Loudmouths and blowhards, take note: Those who beguile and enchant with their deft sense of propriety and interest in others will be easy to promote, difficult to disappoint, and impossible to deny.

RESOURCES

When I need to brush up on my *savoir faire*, I riffle through:

***What Would Jackie Do? An Inspired Guide to Distinctive Living* by Shelly Branch and Sue Callaway**

Branch, Shelly, and Sue Callaway. *What Would Jackie Do? An Inspired Guide to Distinctive Living.*
New York: Gotham Books, 2005.

While Jacqueline Kennedy Onassis was marvelously discrete and circumspect, the authors have talked to her acquaintances and then reimagined Mrs. Onassis as the ultimate role model. From surviving step-parenthood to regifting presents, Mrs. Onassis seems to have had the correct and classy answer to almost all of modern life's challenges. An instructive and fun read for anyone who strives to be a Lady.

***The Power of Nice: How to Conquer the Business World With Kindness* by Linda Kaplan Thaler and Robin Koval**

Kaplan Thaler, Linda, and Robin Koval. *The Power of Nice: How to Conquer the Business World With Kindness.*
New York: Doubleday, 2006.

Call it counterintuitive but two of Madison Avenue's sharpest and savviest chicks have written a book on why "nice" is a marketing strategy. In case you didn't know this, being kind to *all* the men and women in your life (all of them) can benefit you mightily.

. . . and of course . . .

Miss Manners' Guide to Excruciatingly Correct Behavior
by Judith Martin

Martin, Judith. *Miss Manners' Guide to Excruciatingly Correct Behavior.* New York: W. W. Norton & Company, 2005.

Does it matter what you wear to a funeral? Should an adult passenger or should the driver's own child be seated in the front seat of a car? Are preprinted thank-you notes ever acceptable? Finally, a book for those of us who want to know everything that goes into the creation of a flawless, supremely confident presentation. Martin's sharp eye and even sharper writing leaves no doubt that cloddish and selfish behavior, whether it's improperly disposing of a tissue or bringing your (uninvited) children to a party, impacts the way we are perceived.

Fabulous people are competent.

7

Unlike the rest of humanity, who have made *whatever* (not returning phone calls, not answering requests, not turning in work on time) into an art form, there is a type of individual (a.k.a. the Fabulous One) who just loves to outperform and outclass the competition. She will drive you wild with excitement.

Don't you swoon for competence? Aren't you putty in the hands of anyone who really cares about doing things well, consistently? Rather than take the path of least resistance, these intrepid souls tread upon the path of maximum resistance, refusing to cut the corners, drop the balls, and ignore the obvious, even though they can get away with it. These fabulous types relish a post-grad attitude to life: They study books on etiquette, books on sending a great e-mail, books on office politics, books on

Ladies and gentlemen, start your engines!

getting (and keeping) the corner office, books on becoming a leader, books on looking ten years younger—you name it, they're reading it, because being less than stellar is simply not an option worth considering.

WHERE TO START:

In the glorious pursuit of being superb at what you do, may I recommend that you nail the following traits of the Fabulous Ones:

They believe in themselves.

There will always be obstacles to getting ahead, to accomplishing great things, to setting the world on fire. Nobody is kidding themselves—it's a tough world out there, especially if you're holding a full house in the high-stakes game of "high performance." But this is where the truly fabulous eclipse the also-rans: No matter how big the boulder lying across the road, they will get past it and reach their destination. How do you explain this drive and ambition? It boils down to two words: **complete confidence.**

Not a little confidence.

Complete confidence.

This unshakeable belief in one's abilities and talents is the *sine qua non* of the truly competent. Even when the going gets rough, the competent have stockpiled a variety of options to pull them out of the morass. They have friends, allies, colleagues, shrinks, peers, cohorts, mentors, advisors, consultants—even their house painter!—who will listen and/or make suggestions with their best interest at heart.

Furthermore, while they may affect a self-deprecating air, they are keenly aware of what goes into the making of a phenomenon. They did and still do the hard work of figuring it all out—thinking and reflecting, and then writing a list of their talents to refer to in low moments when the chink in their armor becomes like a breached levee. Now they have this list internalized so that every challenge is reframed as an opportunity; every rejection is seen as a wake-up call to strengthen the argument; every defeat is seen as a setback, and nothing more.

Empowered by their own sense of can-do, the competent love the process, the detours, and the distractions that a busy and complicated life will include, but they absolutely will not be outmuscled and outmaneuvered from getting what they want. Why should they second-guess themselves? ***No one else does.***

They are full throttle, all the way!

There's nothing halfway for the competent. They're all in. Whether it's because of their grit factor (they're unafraid to work hard) or their laser-like focus, the truly competent start every day with a morning cocktail of discovery and excitement, a drink so potent it should be bottled and sold to every aspiring leader.

This ability to be "on" is what makes someone a star.

You've experienced it, I'm sure. You are standing in a room and suddenly someone walks in practically vibrating with purpose and excitement and, suddenly, you are more energized, more alert. Their personal energy, the buoyancy in their walk, raises the temperature in the room (and thank God for that!), or so they make you feel. Actually, nothing has changed in the room except *your* perspective about the possibilities.

See, here's what you need to understand: These competent types are convinced of their capabilities so they do not permit the underminers and second-guessers lurking in the background to dilute or derail their trajectories. When they say they're going to do something, they do it. They bring the same level of intensity to every rung on the ladder of success.

For the truly competent, giving 1,000 percent to everything they do is second nature. Occasionally, perhaps when they haven't had enough sleep, they may use the "whatever" word, but never as a declaration of indifference. They've figured out that the only way to maximize their enjoyment is to maximize their commitment and go full throttle. That's why their names are in the top five on many a speed dial.

They are shamelessly, exuberantly, absolutely *loco* about life.

I'm going to give it to you straight: The truly competent are having more fun than the rest of us. Because when you love what you do and you happen to be very, very good at it, life is exciting. And if these competent types don't love what they are doing (and haven't for awhile), they are not ashamed to ask for help. They reach out to their mentors, their friends, and their colleagues, and they brainstorm the various avenues they need to explore in order to feel empowered and productive.

Oh sure, once in a while they'll get balled up and start to remember the days when their trajectory was influenced by anxiety and insecurity, but those days are *done-zo*. Now all they need to do is just focus on the next big hurrah, the next big mountain to climb.

Top Performers

Top performers are a different breed. I've had the great fortune to coach high performers and this is what they've taught me about excelling in life:

Top performers are wonderful at creating a memorable first impression. They understand the subtleties of working their verbal and nonverbal signals to telegraph their availability, interest in others, and appetite for life.

Top performers enjoy what they are doing. They're passionate about their purpose. They move through setbacks with resolve. Don't misunderstand me; these people have had their share of curveballs. The difference is that they learned when to swing and when to duck.

Top performers look good. We're not talking beauty contests here—but a polished, supremely confident appearance enhances their power and persuasive abilities. They use their packaging wisely.

Top performers think like racecar drivers. They know they can accelerate into a curve, using the car's momentum for control and velocity. They move forward with confidence and competence, giving life everything they've got.

Top performers are excellent communicators. They're gifted listeners. They're adept at separating the context from the content. They welcome dissent. And most importantly, they're fully present so the speaker feels respected and acknowledged.

Top performers inspire collegiality and cooperation. They empower others to achieve and be the best at what they do. They're unafraid of showing their true authentic self, warts and all.

And finally, **top performers** are fun to be with. They filter life's vicissitudes through the lens of irony, humor, jest, and a healthy dollop of self-deprecation. They work hard and they laugh even harder. It's no wonder they're at the top of their game.

Go Ahead; Seduce Me!

Want to know what I find seductive in both men and women? It's not beauty, money, brains, style, or long-stemmed roses. It's **competence**. I love when someone says they're going to do something and does it! (Makes my heart race.) I love when someone confirms the receipt of an e-mail. (Makes me weak in the knees.) I love . . .

. . . when someone writes me an e-mail that not only acknowledges my question or statement but follows it up with a complete, legible, spell-checked response.

. . . people that show up on time for an appointment. To me, that communicates respect for my time as well as their own.

. . . short voicemail messages that get right to the point. All I need to hear is the date, time, and reason for the call. And leave your phone number.

. . . documents that are attached or embedded in the e-mail. In fact, attach the documents *before* you start writing to ensure that you won't forget to do it.

. . . people who return my phone calls within twenty-four hours.

. . . proactive, high-energy types that pick up a phone when an e-mail request has not been answered, rather than stew and complain.

. . . people who try to figure things out for themselves before asking for help. Between Google, Yahoo, and Wikipedia, we should all think before we question.

. . . hearing from old friends, but please identify yourself by your full name on the voicemail rather than, "Hi, it's me."

. . . a proper introduction that includes my name and my company affiliation whenever I'm meeting a client or a colleague. We should toot our own horn as well as those of the people we work with.

. . . crisp, well-organized notes after a meeting has taken place that not only document what was discussed but detail the action steps that need to be taken.

. . . people with the confidence and the competence to have a meeting or a conversation without being interrupted by incessantly trilling cell phones or BlackBerries. *Now that's seductive.*

And here's something else you ought to know: The fun is evident the minute you're in their force field. Completely engaged and emotionally generous, they know they are casting a potent spell with their mastery, intellectual vigor, and plain-out lustiness, and they use that incandescence to illuminate a life rife with possibilities.

They are driven by a need to get things done.

There is a reason that competent people accomplish so much. First of all, they want their lives to matter. Secondly, they're driven by a pronounced sense of "purpose," something so overwhelming they are willing to put themselves on the line in order to get it done.

Purpose encourages risk—taking a chance, calling someone for support, reinventing your fashion look—and discovering that the easiest way to recharge your batteries is to just keep setting higher goals. Having a purpose will also stave off the blues, the sense of despair that everyone experiences when work becomes tedious and life is inexorably predictable. Maybe purpose's purpose is to remind us that as long as we believe in something bigger than ourselves, we'll always be optimistic and positive in our thinking.

Having a purpose is more than just making money and getting the leased car. The truly competent want their lives to mean something. They want it to matter. It might come early in their years or later on but all of us have the capacity to make a difference in someone's life. And if you haven't found your purpose, that's it: Every day, find a way to make a difference in someone else's life. Visit a sick neighbor; try your hand at matchmaking. Even if you don't take home a trophy, someone else will feel like a winner.

Opportunities Galore

For those who master the essential elements of a professional presence, there will be opportunities galore. Here's how I'd leave the rest of the world *in the dust*:

- **Opportunity 1: First impressions count and they're impossible to erase.** Once perceived as a dud, always seen as a dud. Don't underestimate how much power you have over perception. Go for broke: Smartly tailored clothes that befit your work situation, hairstyles that are sleek and polished, and accessories that are memorable, give you an edge.

- **Opportunity 2: Manners matter.** I love when someone stands to offer a handshake, holds the door an extra second, says "excuse me" when they step on my foot, admonishes their child to refrain from wrecking a storefront window, and says "good morning" even when they don't know me.

- **Opportunity 3: E-mail can brand you as a superperformer,** if you observe a few cardinal rules. Always create a subject line to reflect the topic of the e-mail. Make that subject line irresistible so it gets opened before the others. (Aside: Do not go all haywire and change the subject line's meaning if you're writing back and forth on a specific project at work.) Attach the document when you refer to the document. Don't send mass mailings unless you're confident we're interested in your latest obsession.

- **Opportunity 4: Voicemail messages should be to the point.** That means name, number, tightly edited purpose of the call, and a repeat of the phone number. Free association works on the analytic couch, not while we're catching up with messages.

- **Opportunity 5: "Outbehave your competition."** That's what Dov Seidman writes in his book *How*. How you engage with others, how you collaborate, and how you apologize when you drop a greasy spoon on my lap, is what sets you apart.

- **Opportunity 6: Banish "whatever."** Don't think it, don't say it, and don't act it out. Everything matters.

- **Opportunity 7: Toot your own horn.** Products die on the shelf without consistent promotion, and talented individuals are ignored or not utilized without effective self-promotion. No matter what is going on in your life, lead with enthusiasm, vigor, and a few choice sound bites about what you're working on.

- **Opportunity 8: Don't mumble.** Sit up straight, throw your shoulders back, and articulate.

- **Opportunity 9: Know something.** Movies, theater, music, opera, museums, galleries, travel spots, personal trainer, tailor, nutritionist, designer, advertising guru . . . be generous with information. It brands you as a leader.

- **Opportunity 10: Eschew shortcuts.** Send a handwritten note instead of an e-mail. Keep an iron handy to touch up the collars of your shirts. Engage with the salesclerk before handing over the credit card, and introduce people before starting a meeting.

Opportunities to show panache rarely fall into the lap. Be creative.

Be Different

Recently, I opened a catalogue from a store in Charleston called Ben Silver. The catalogue is filled with nifty clothes and accessories, from saddle shoes to horn-rim glasses to bowties. As I was leafing through it, I thought to myself, "Gee, if someone showed up wearing saddle shoes, I bet they'd stand out."

In this great big virtual world in which there are no secretaries to sweet-talk into putting your message in the front of the pile, and in which a job listing can elicit thousands of responses, how do you get noticed?

The road to being different starts with confidence. Don't wait for someone to hand it to you—hand it to yourself. Acknowledge your gifts, your talents, your originality, and work it! Success is a trajectory, a direction that you control with positive expectations of yourself and your capabilities. By setting your compass in the direction of high performance, you can well afford to take advantage of all the subtle details that make someone memorable. Great manners do it. Sharply written communication does it. A flair for self-presentation nails it. Everything must be working in sync to ensure that when you enter a room or leave a message, a positive aura surrounds you:

- Blatant, in-your-face enthusiasm is a great barometer to your self-esteem. A great attitude about life's curveballs will endear you to others and leave a deep impression upon everyone you meet.
- An e-mail's subject line is the headline to your story. Don't overlook this introduction to your own personal style by neglecting to change it or even worse, going for the obvious, like, "Hi."

- With everyone claiming attention deficit disorder, the chances of getting to paragraph 2 in a letter or note are increasingly small. Use the first sentence to stop the reader with a snappy and bold declaration or exhortation!

- Every time you walk out the door, you're advertising. If you're selling luxury, and by that I mean high performance, you'd better look luxurious.

- The cool, laidback persona is on the wane. Today the buzzword is passion. Do you have it? Nothing is more persuasive or memorable than someone who really believes in themselves, their company, or their product, and wears their heart on their sleeve.

- Be different. If everyone gets sloppy in the summer and wears creased chinos with a barely pressed shirt, go all out and wear the crispest, sharpest pants with an equally "spit and polish" long-sleeved shirt and tie. If your coworkers are treading on thin ice with bare shoulders and cropped pants, upstage them with perfectly fitted pants suits or a terrific skirt, camisole, and lightweight sweater or jacket.

Cutting a wide swath and going for unforgettable can be very addictive. Trust me.

They are unafraid to ask for H-E-L-P!

A wise man *(all right, it was my shrink)* told me, "No one can read your mind." And it's true—none of us are psychics (including the people with PSYCHIC on their business card) so you've got to tell people what you need so they can give you the support and, if necessary, the props to get there.

You see, the competent are not arrogant. They know they can't get to where they want to go *all by themselves.* They know their limitations and they accept them, and they also know that whatever it is they don't know, someone else does.

So they master the art of persuasion. They adopt a style of speaking that's rich and potent in its enthusiasm and passion. They talk about what they're doing with a kind of immediacy and intimacy that enables people to feel the excitement. This encourages people to get involved and take part in their dreams so that when the going gets rough, they are there to offer help or support. And when the going does get rough, they're smart—they know who to call when they have questions or concerns, and they're fearless about picking up the phone and asking someone for more brainpower.

And get this: The competent are not afraid of being outsmarted. They're not keeping score. In fact, there's nothing they like better than to meet someone smarter, someone with an extra piece of mental energy that they can access. (How do you think they got so competent in the first place?)

They are reliably consistent. *(Sigh.)*

It's one thing to do something really well once or twice. But to do it over and over again requires the mindset of a true professional—someone who holds himself to the highest of standards and produces the kind of work that is not only reliable but consistently excellent. Someone you can count on.

To achieve that level of excellence you need to take your work very seriously and understand how everything you do really does matter. Whatever it is you do, give it the respect and honor it deserves. You could be a hairstylist, a plastic surgeon, or a plumber—it doesn't matter. What matters is that each time you approach a task, you apply the same level of detail that you did the first time.

Just think about it: Every time you step onto a plane, you expect the pilot to bring you safely to your destination. Your life depends on the pilot getting it right, adjusting the wings, making sure all the engines are running in tip-top shape. Why should it be any different for those whose job it is to deliver a report, fill an order, or look perfectly polished day after day? It's this consistency, the ability to deliver superior results over and over again, that defines the superstar . . . or in your case, the fabulous.

WANT TO GO FOR IT?

To telegraph an unmistakable aura of competence:

1. **Establish authority by creating a memorable first impression.** Master the subtleties of verbal and nonverbal signals to communicate your enthusiasm in the world at large. Pay close attention to your image (clothing), your personal grooming, and your enthusiastic attitude to ensure that everything works in sync—what you look like, what you say, and how you say it.

2. **Now, overdeliver.** Don't kid yourself—no one can resist the person who consistently, willingly (and cheerfully) does more than the minimum. Forget about the idea of "slack" and how much you should get or want. The genius of competence is mastering the details: returning your phone calls; sending a link to an article that can benefit someone else's business; confirming appointments, and including street address and emergency cell phone numbers in case of a snafu; turning in the work on time and then without a nudge or a poke, moving ahead to the next project.

3. **Be flexible.** Someone who's truly competent is unafraid of trying something new, even if it means feeling lost and uncertain.

RESOURCES

We should all be perennial students and I'm not ashamed to hit the books when I need to raise my grade:

Brag! The Art of Tooting Your Own Horn by Peggy Klaus

Klaus, Peggy. *Brag! The Art of Tooting Your Own Horn.* New York: Warner Business Books, 2003.

Do people know that you're good at what you do? Have you nailed your "elevator speech"—the 10-second introduction you give of yourself—or do you sell yourself short? In this crazy, hyperdistracted world, you cannot afford to miss even one opportunity to demonstrate your competence. Klaus shows how to create "sound bites" about your latest accomplishment so you can talk about yourself in a way that's unaffected yet compels people to regard you with admiration.

Shakespeare in Charge: The Bard's Guide to Leading and Succeeding on the Business Stage **by Norman Augustine and Kenneth Adelman**

Augustine, Norman, and Kenneth Adelman. *Shakespeare in Charge: The Bard's Guide to Leading and Succeeding on the Business Stage.* New York: Hyperion, 1999.

Like Jane Austen, who illustrated human folly through her perfectly rendered characters, William Shakespeare is the ultimate business guru for aspiring leaders who seek wisdom and insight in managing and motivating people through crisis and change.

Fabulous people just "get it."

8

We don't talk enough about the *get it* factor, so let's do it right now. By far the most subtle aspect of someone's fabulousness, the *get it* factor, is like a perfect newsboy cap in glen plaid (worn with a short raincoat and driving gloves, yes?). Just a little detail, to be sure, but, boy, talk about making an impact! Spend time with someone who gets it or who's *with-it* and you don't need to explain everything. These virtuosos can switch gears. From Ellen on *Idol* to Krugman on Larry Summers, they're ambidextrous conversationalists without a whit of snobbishness. Hey, Joan Didion admits to reading *The Enquirer* and she's as high-brow as it gets . . . but that's what makes her, well, you know, *fabulous.*

Besides being plugged in to the cultural zeitgeist, people who get it are emotionally attuned. Their level of empathy and compassion is born out of a deep understanding of the human spirit. They use their powers of observation and their gut-level instincts to make informed judgments about other people's feelings. And when someone is in need, they don't wait for that person to call and ask for help. They call or write or just

Everyone Is Smart

Smart once ruled the world. You toddled, prepped, and earned the diploma at the marquee school. Your future was set. You could do anything and go anywhere.

Sorry. It's not like that anymore.

Today *everyone* is smart. If you have Internet access and some curiosity, you're brilliant. Technical know-how (like good looks) can dazzle but it will only get you so far. You need something more. The big opportunities come to those who can sell themselves.

In a cutthroat, underemployment-is-the-name-of-the-game world, you need to figure out what makes you exceptional, write the narrative, and go out and sell it. No hemming and hawing—this is high-stakes sales, which requires fully deployed showmanship:

- Start the day convinced you'll close every deal. The little tape inside your head should loop the most flattering, motivating messages day and night. Delete messages that undermine your sense of worth and confidence. (Leave that to your frenemies.)
- Show up for work looking like a million bucks. When you're expecting success, you get it.
- Talk up your product. We're listening; intrigue us with a story or an anecdote that makes us root for you.
- Old-fashioned good manners are the cornerstone of the most luxurious. Return your phone calls, update people on the viability of their proposals, keep us posted.
- Word-of-mouth is how great products catch fire, so nourish your horizontal relationships (peers, colleagues, friends, cohorts). Do I really need to remind you that no one gets to the top of Everest without a sherpa?
- Smarts, savvy, competence—all good. Top it off with exuberance and passion, and I'm signing on the dotted line.

jump in the car because they know that their efforts will be both mood elevating and therapeutic.

There's a reason people escape to their cell phone screen when seated next to a stranger: They're terrified of being held captive to a bore. Or even worse than a bore, someone who doesn't care about anything except his or her own life. Those of us who live our lives with gusto and pride ourselves on absorbing it all are always on the lookout for someone who can mesmerize us with conversational hairpin turns and intellectual hijinks. And by the way, this has nothing to do with SAT scores or where or if you went to college. These modern-day Scheherazades are literate. They listen (more than they talk!) They are open to people who are not like them. They go to theater and the movies and listen to Paul Simon *and* Grizzly Bear. They're fascinated by everything and they're relentless about being hip to the zeitgeist. That's what makes them exhilarating to be with; they're with you all the way.

HERE'S WHAT THEY DO:

They remain open.

What a drag to sit next to someone whose reference points are so dated. Like bad milk, some people reach their expiration point way too soon. To be completely with-it, you need to have a mind that's willing to be challenged and unafraid of being wrong. The most exciting conversationalists are the people whose minds are not made up . . . who would die before saying, "Well, in my day . . . " (In the words of Nora Ephron, "Who cares what happened in your day? It's not your day anymore.") And while they hold passionate opinions, they are always willing to debate an issue and see it from a new vantage point—*even if the vantage point forces them to question their preconceived notions.*

With-it-ness connotes a kind of intellectual vibrancy, an insatiable curiosity about a myriad of topics. Like the Renaissance men before us who pursued multiple fields of study, such as philosophy, art, engineering, and foreign languages, staying open to learning is the hallmark of the totally fabulous.

They teach themselves new tricks.

When my friend's eighty-plus-year-old husband made a reference to Facebook, I did a double swoon. Don't you absolutely love it when someone who could be complaining about a hip replacement is instead just totally and completely hip?

That's the goal, my friends.

Forget your age and force yourself to stay *au courant.* Whatever is in vogue, whether it's getting onto Twitter or texting, go out and learn it or find someone to teach you how to do it. Go to Google and type in "What's on Jay-Z's iPod?" and download the songs that resonate. Buy a smartphone and learn how to customize it so that it acts like a personal assistant. Listen to Pavement and when in L.A. head up to Malibu and eat at a roadside shack, not at some haute place mentioned in the late (and sorely missed) *Gourmet.*

The point I'm trying to make—and it's a big one—is this: Never lose the passion and the zest for acquiring information. Don't be satisfied with what you know. Keep learning and dreaming and challenging yourself. Life is exciting but it's *you* who makes it exciting. Don't rest on your laurels; don't be afraid of looking foolish. Learning and experimenting

It's fun to talk to someone who doesn't suffer from myopia.

ASIA
CHINA
JAPAN
NORTH PA
OCEAN

How to Appear Hipper Than You Really Are

- Yes, I know, thongs are annoyingly uncomfortable but that VPL (visible panty line) makes you look very old.
- You can watch *Masterpiece Theater* and still know that Chris Brown beat up Rihanna.
- Very few will listen to a voicemail message from beginning to end.
- In fact, don't even bother leaving a message. Your name/number says it all.
- If you're on e-mail, respond within 12 hours. Otherwise admit it: You "have" e-mail but you don't use it.
- Have a presence on Facebook, but no photographs of yourself looking kinda creepy and, God forbid, crepey.
- Break fashion rules left and right. White jeans in the winter look amazingly hip.
- Lower your voice when speaking on a cell phone.
- Don't talk about your kids.
- Prunes vs. Metamucil: *Too much information!*

and even falling short of your goals is all part of the process of being alive. And most importantly, the thing to remember when you're on a quest to teach yourself new tricks is to remember that you're not going to look dumb; you're going to look courageous, no matter whether you succeed or fail. So forget the needles of Botox and the syringes filled with collagen. The modern way to stay young and vibrant is to keep your mind razor sharp. The secret:

They read, study, and absorb everything.

With-it-ness takes work. Every day, you need to read a newspaper cover to cover, whether you're reading the paper version or the online one—Sports, Business, International, and the Obituaries. (Why not? Those obits can be epic.)

Read fiction and nonfiction, and even if you don't have time to read a book cover to cover, you need to know who won this year's Pulitzer.

Becoming fabulous means taking a huge interest in the world around you—everything, including *New Yorker* cartoons, Dowd and Collins at *The Times,* as well as what killed Michael Jackson. It means you can't just be interested in the stuff that interests you—you've got to be interested in the stuff that interests *me* so that when we get together it's fun to tickle each other's minds with scintillating chat.

Just for fun, read the top Web aggregators like Huffington Post or the Daily Beast, or highly specialized and navel-picking sites like Nikki Finke's Deadline Hollywood Daily. These topical Web sites cover everything from politics to celebrities, and they're always up to date on breaking news. It's amazing how a little inside dope on Jeff Zucker's terror reign at NBC can make you seem like such a player.

Challenge yourself to stay abreast of topics that leave you utterly bewildered, whether it's the newest stars in the hip-hop firmament or the politics behind the aggressiveness in women's soccer. Start slowly so that you're getting acquainted with the buzzwords and the personalities that dominate the subject. I promise you, one day you'll be sitting next to someone quite attractive who will want to talk about just that topic, and there you are, ready to share your very educated opinion. (Oh, how fabulous you're going to feel!)

RESOURCES

At times I'm admittedly dense when it comes to "the moment." You simply cannot consider yourself "plugged in" by reading one newspaper, so why not spend a few minutes reading the Web sites that aggregate the provocative and fascinating stories that are dominating the news cycle? My personal favorites include:

www.rollingstone.com

For those of us who want to stay hip to the zeitgeist but have been known to say "50 Cents" when referring to a certain superstar.

www.deadlinehollywooddaily.com

Nikki Finke's lacerating wit and ferocious reporting skills are on full display in this marvelous read on the business, the personalities, and the money that rules Hollywood.

www.politico.com

Up and running in time to catch the wave of excitement of the 2008 election, this Web site still breaks stories, leaks memos, and makes daily newspapers quiver with fear at their nimbleness and relevancy.

www.nytimes.com

I don't care what anybody says—I still get a frisson of excitement when I open my front door and find the *Times* sitting on my driveway. But I get it: You're perfectly content to read it online. Columnists Maureen Dowd (Wed. & Sun.); Gail Collins (Thurs. & Sat.); David Brooks (Tues. & Fri.); and three-time Pulitzer Prize–winner Tom Friedman (Wed. & Sun.), as well as business reporters Andrew Ross Sorkin and David Carr, are not to be missed.

www.newyorker.com

Even if you can't plow through the entire issue, the cultural listings, "Talk of the Town," Roz Chast's cartoons, and Anthony Lane's film reviews are worth the price of admission.

Fabulous people have a big bandwidth.

9

How big is your bandwidth? I'm serious.

Can you talk, with equal engagement and respect, to your company's CFO *and* the guy who pumps your gas? Can you connect with someone whose background is completely different from yours? Are you comfortable out of your circle or do you dread going anywhere where you won't be hanging with your posse?

That's the essence of a big, juicy (lucrative) bandwidth: the range of people you can build a relationship with, not because they went to your college, golf at your club, or worship at the same church, mosque, or synagogue, but because you've found the common thread, the place where everything fades away except for your mutual admiration and interest in each other.

The truly fabulous don't need a comfort zone that excludes and limits contact with people who are different from them. It's just the opposite. Their curiosity and appetite for amusing and provocative conversation requires talking to a lot of people with a myriad of backgrounds, experiences, and points of view. That's why they're great conversationalists . . . because the scope of their interests is so broad.

WHERE TO START:

How do the fabulous ones maintain such a broad bandwidth?

They are master initiators.

In addition to being talented communicators and world-class listeners, these socially ebullient types are supremely good at building relationships, using their entire bodies to communicate complete respect and interest in others. They do not multitask, they look someone in the eye (and not over their shoulders, which suggests they're hoping for someone more important to enter the room), and they understand the value of giving someone their full attention.

Like all top performers, they are always *on*, to ensure they're not missing anything. They listen to everything lest they miss the moment when they can share and empathize. Coupled with a gift for intuition—an ability to pick up on a mood that even the speaker may be unaware of—their talent for multilevel listening enables them to move from the lightheartedly superficial into the kind of smart talk that fosters real friendship and intimacy.

And that, of course, explains why they have black belts in networking.

In case you didn't know this already, networking has nothing to do with handing out business cards or getting a name to contact, and *everything* to do with meeting interesting people and acquiring useful information. That's why the big-bandwidth boys and girls are eagerly collecting a treasure trove of tips, hints, ideas, and suggestions from a wide circle of sources.

You see, these fabulous types have experienced something the rest of us are just figuring out: The bigger the bandwidth, the bigger the influence, the bigger the fun.

They want everyone to win.

People with big bandwidths are more fun to play with because of their genuine interest in other people's success. Believe it or not, some people get a real *kick* out of seeing people move ahead. And because they're all things fabulous, they also know *how* to help people get ahead.

Driven by this (at times) feverish desire to see other people achieve, the socially fearless are occasionally forced to do big, bold things like set up a meeting, arrange an interview, or write a letter of recommendation. They will even go out on a limb and request a favor. They know the rules of asking (never from someone who cannot gratify the request, since they might end up making that person feel weak and impotent). They weren't always this confident, surely not. They've had moments when they didn't know when to ask or who to ask, and so they held back and, frankly, languished on the sidelines while other people just picked up the phone and took care of what needed to get done. Then, eureka! The fabulous realized that if they had kept score (which they hadn't), they would have figured out that they have given a lot more than they have *received.* That was the turning point.

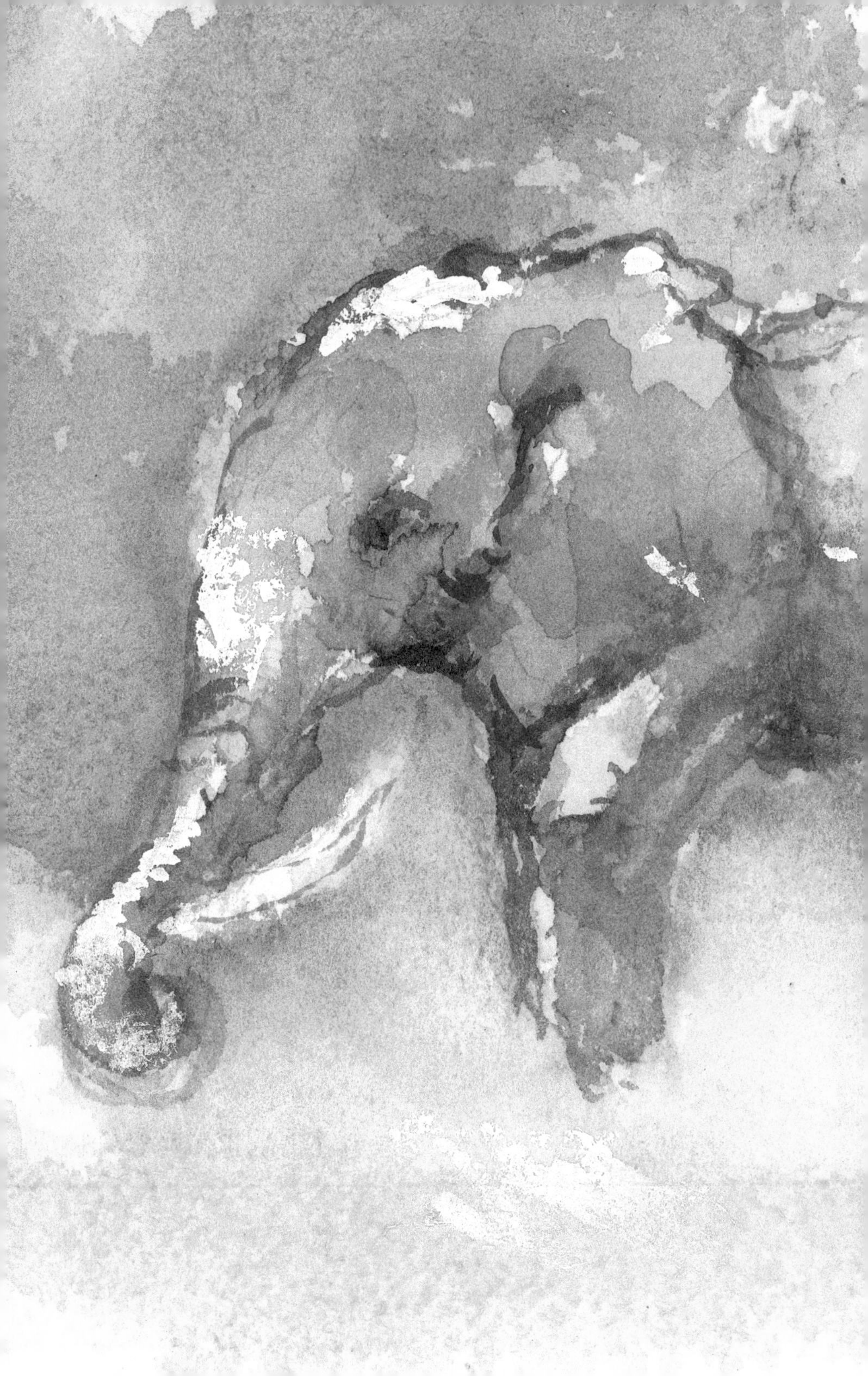

They could now stop dragging their feet when they (or someone else) needed something, and just get on with it. In other words: Ask for the help, damnit! It's not the end of the world to request a favor.

Are you wondering, "Why do it? Why go out of your way to see someone else succeed?"

Because the Fabulous One would be the first to tell you: *Someone did it for me.* And fabulous types have memories like elephants. They never forget.

They are socially adept.

It's not our fault. No one taught us how to be social gazelles. Did anyone take you aside and say, "If you enter a party and see not one familiar face, make a beeline to two people talking to one another and wait patiently for a lull in the conversation and just stick out your hand and say, 'Hi, I'm Diana and I've never come to one of these (take your pick: party, networking event, inner-circle confab). May I join you in the conversation?'" (Of course no one taught us this stuff. Our mothers were too busy waxing the floor and folding laundry.)

Imagine how confident we would be if, from an early age, we learned how to escape a "close talker" the same way we practiced writing declarative sentences in a paragraph. (Hint: Move two steps back as if you're trying to regain your balance.) What if, in addition to mastering multiplication and long division, we had mastered the gift of meaningful gab?

Fabulous people have elephantine memory banks. Of course they remember the slights, but they're especially good at remembering the high fives.

(Hint: Superficial topics that seem to resonate with most include traffic patterns, how to lower cholesterol, and whether dogs should wear cashmere sweaters.)

Since no one can do a better job of explaining the fundamentals of working a room better than Jeanne Martinet, I beseech you to read *The Art of Mingling,* a first-class primer on breaking and entering any social milieu. Martinet has the mechanics of chitchat and hobnobbing down to a science. But while Martinet focuses mainly on the dread factor (which is the only true impediment to going out and having a blast, no matter where you are), here's my way of looking at socializing: It's an opportunity to meet someone who can put some zip in your life!

Take advantage of every opportunity to get in front of smart, wonderful people. This is why you've done all the work on your confidence. This is why your attitude intrigues and enchants. This is why you've developed a repertoire of imaginative things to talk about: so you can walk into any room and dazzle all present with your accessibility, engaging charm, and nonstop humor.

Make it clear that you're interested in what other people have to say. Listen and follow up with questions. Take the lead in introducing people to one another, and don't wait for your host to ensure Tom meets Harry. Introduce them yourself, and make sure you have something to say about Tom that would be of interest to Harry (and vice versa) to move that relationship along. And *no.* You do not start a conversation by talking about yourself and your annual vacation at the Hotel du Cap. (We're just feigning interest when you do.)

And for goodness' sake, be on the lookout for someone who

How to Excel at Small Talk

- Small talk's strength comes from observation. Study someone and get a sense of who they are before engaging in conversation.
- Look for details on someone's presentation style to get started. Two-color wing tips, oversized cameos, a wide Pucci-inspired headband may be indications of someone who would welcome your questions and your interest.
- Since everyone loves to talk about him- or herself, start the ball rolling with unintrusive questions. The purpose of small talk is to get someone to loosen up.
- Afraid of being provocative? Nothing beats, "So what do you think of those Mets/Knicks/Red Sox?" Or, you could ask, "How do you spend your leisure time?"
- Observant conversation is only half the battle; the other half is paying full attention to someone's answers, which can act as a bridge to more indepth talk. "Wow, I didn't know they were teaching Latin in kindergarten."
- Gossip is not small talk. However, character analysis about a well-known personality is a good starting point. "I wasn't surprised to hear that his show wasn't renewed. I heard he was impossible to work with . . . "
- Staying *au courant* when it comes to theater, movies, sports, the stock market, and travel will enable you to talk to just about anybody.
- Having said that, there are going to be people who pride themselves on living in a cave without any access to the world. Do not despair; you can always ask them about their first car and its mileage before they traded it in.
- If that fails, ask someone if they've ever eaten kale. Everyone has an opinion about kale.

The Realm's New Currency

How big is your bandwidth?

Evidently John Donahue, president of eBay, has a very big one. In a recent article in the *New York Times*, Thomas Tierney, an eBay director, said Mr. Donahue has "an uncanny ability to connect with everyone, from receptionists to chief executives. Getting along socially and being able to build relationships is a type of social bandwidth that is hard to come by." By giving Donahue high marks, Tierney was making the point that the range of people you can successfully communicate with (social bandwidth) is more important to leadership than technical know-how.

Ben Silverman, former cochairman of NBC's entertainment division, is also one of the premier networkers in Los Angeles, a town where relationships often define success. No one seemed surprised when NBC hired the former television producer (*The Office*), since according to the *Times*, "Silverman has international relationships unmatched everywhere."

Social bandwidth, relationships, and emotional intelligence are the new currency of the realm. If you're deficient in those areas, you're cooked. The annoying habits of hyperdistractedness and CrackBerry addiction, poor communication skills, and bad attitude, can derail even the most accomplished. There's only one remedy to bad social skills: good social skills. Here's how to approach the new and improved you:

- **Treat everyone with respect.** I respect people for the way they treat the shoeshine guy, the parking lot attendant, and the boss. It all matters.
- **Be an active listener.** Don't step on my lines, finish my thoughts, or habitually ask me for the "short" version.
- **Stop whining.** Don't disparage the competition. In fact, don't disparage anyone. Earn a reputation for staying optimistic, no matter what the challenges.
- **Smile more.** A top performer who wears a smile instead of a scowl builds teamwork and allegiance.
- **Look for opportunities to praise and nurture.** Most people are ignored and overlooked, whether at work or at home. Acknowledge their talents.
- **Initiate a hello.** People who extend their hand and introduce themselves in any situation (meeting, networking event, cafeteria line) win.
- **Encourage other people.** An authentic leader is not the one who occupies the corner office but rather the person who takes pleasure in other people's success.
- **Make eye contact.** I'm not talking "the window to the soul." I'm talking about deepening the connection and the relationships that enlarge your life, never mind your bandwidth.

is standing by himself and find a way to include him in a conversation. You never know—this stranger could be the person you've been hoping to meet your entire life.

WANT TO GO FOR IT?

To channel your inner whirling dervish:

1. **Stop second-guessing yourself.** Maximize your enjoyment of life by jettisoning the caustic and nonsensical thoughts that float through your mind and end up undermining your power and optimistic attitude. Upload that personal sound loop and listen to it gleefully, joyfully, and believe in it. Go out thinking you are the most dazzling creature on the planet. Trust me: A steady stream of self-directed compliments is marvelous to listen to and will put you in the proper mindset to meet interesting and compelling new people.

2. Yeah, yeah, all the books tell you to eat some protein before attending a party but **don't forget to read that day's newspaper**, too, so you have something to talk about besides your job, your kids, or your diet. The most captivating conversationalists are world-class listeners who are genuinely interested in hearing about someone's life. They are also voracious readers with a talent for remembering details.

3. Shyness update: Most people are terrified of being in a situation where they don't see a familiar face, so **view every social situation as an opportunity to show off your newfound poise and assurance.** Smile at everyone. Introduce people to each other. Don't offer a hand that's cold and wet from an icy drink (dry it off first!) And

seek out opportunities to meet new people face-to-face because no matter how often you text and tweet, nothing takes the place of sharing a laugh or a confidence.

RESOURCES

Even a hostess with the mostest can get a refresher course in exploiting life's mundane moments by reading:

What to Say When You Talk to Your Self by Shad Helmstetter

Helmstetter, Shad. *What to Say When You Talk to Your Self.* New York: Pocket Books, 1982.

I know, we're not supposed to blame Mommy, but how else to explain that voice in our head admonishing us for spilling the coffee and forgetting what's-his-name's name? *What to Say When You Talk to Your Self* will help you reprogram your inner soundtrack so that you're listening to a steady stream of affirming and validating commentary about why you're special. Imagine, if you will, an entire day spent in the company of someone who thinks you're delightful, delicious, delectable, delirious—and clearly de-lovely. Who wouldn't feel and act like they had the world on a string?

The Art of Mingling: Easy, Fun, and Proven Techniques for Mastering Any Room by Jeanne Martinet

Martinet, Jeanne. *The Art of Mingling: Easy, Fun, and Proven Techniques for Mastering Any Room.* New York: St. Martin's Griffin, 2006.

You need to understand: Most of us are tongue-tied at parties. Plunging into a room full of strangers is intimidating; coming up with the clever riposte at just the right moment is daunting if not impossible. But author Martinet has taken all the anxiety out of mingling by breaking it down to its simplest components: the introductions; the small talk; how to flatter; and of course, the most effective ways to "get away" from someone who's a low talker, close talker, or dull talker.

Masters of Networking: Building Relationships for Your Pocketbook and Soul **by Ivan R. Misner and Don Morgan**

Misner, Ivan, and Don Morgan. *Masters of Networking: Building Relationships for Your Pocketbook and Soul.*
Atlanta: Bard Press, 2000.

Would you be surprised to learn that the reason Colin Powell is one of the world's top networkers is that he's smart, sincere, and delightful to spend time with? The masters of networking are not glib or sycophantic or willing to jump over the family heirlooms in order to get what they want. *Au contraire*: People who are superior at networking are information junkies with a prodigious memory that enables them to pull out the information when it's appropriate and give it to someone who can use it. In other words, these masters are hard-wired for giving, not getting. It's well worth reading how some of the world's most successful people use their best selves to widen their nets.

10

Fabulous people are vivid virtually.

You mustn't hide fabulousness. Even in a world where practically everything is virtual, the authentic and fabulous self must come through. It doesn't matter the medium—sender box, caller I.D., the back of an envelope—you must have a presence so that the moment your name appears, the receiver experiences a *jolt* of anticipation.

However you prefer to communicate, your sense of aplomb, mastery of tone, and (let's not forget) ability to write a coherent sentence, must be crisply apparent, leaving no doubt that you are worth listening to. Come on . . . does anything else matter?

WHERE TO START:

Developing a superior virtual presence requires a mastery of several mediums—phone, e-mail, text messaging, and let's not forget handwritten notes—but the payoff is undeniable. No longer will you be lumped in with all the drab and dreary e-mails that get lost in the thicket or the phone calls that are sent to voicemail (and never returned). To break through the wall and create a virtual image so vivid it's practically palpable, you must show some flair and originality when communicating, but take it seriously too. Watch for grammar, typos, and slurred voicemails. And know when to e-mail, when to call, and when only a handwritten note will do.

Allow me to show you how the fabulous get it right, meduim by medium:

E-MAILS

They know that e-mails are letters.

Where did we get the distorted idea that e-mails were not letters? They are letters! Little letters, big letters, sometimes even mean-spirited letters, but they are most definitely letters (but without postage). One-word answers? Surely you jest. Send me an e-mail with the answer "Sure" in response to my question, and I will get lost in the thicket of e-mail unintelligibility, worrying that I've somehow overstepped my bounds or annoyed you with my request.

Admit it: We all know what we're going to get (a.k.a. "the payoff") the minute we see someone's name in our inbox. That's what branding is all about. Just by seeing your name (never mind the subject line . . . we'll get to that in a minute), we know whether we're going to be titillated or bored, intrigued or indifferent, maybe even amused or annoyed. We even know if you're going to respond to our response. People, we know a lot of stuff about you by the way you e-mail. Can you really afford to look less than fabulous?

Like all letters, e-mails require an intro sentence . . . a greeting ("I hope this e-mail finds you in great spirits" or "Yo,

Bill, what's happening?"), the point of the e-mail, and then a closing sentence ("I appreciate your help" or "When can I see you?"). They also require a closing salutation, like "Warmest regards" or if you're smoochy in style, "XXOO." In between the opening and closing sentences, shoot for something clever and charming. Why not? It takes the same amount of time and it decreases the chances of being dropped to the bottom of the list or, worse, being told, "Oops. It probably went to my SPAM box." (Really. The stories people tell us when they really ought to say, "Please punch up the subject line so that I know it's a **guaranteed good time**.")

Ah, the subject line. Also known as the headline or catchy title. I cannot overstate why you must labor over the subject line to flag our attention. Anyone who lives a normal life has way too much e-mail so you've got to be merciless. Forget "hi" and "re: (blank)." You have choices. Either alert the reader that the message is time-sensitive ("URGENT") or captivate us with its upbeat originality ("I was on my way home when . . . ")

Happily, for those of us pressed for time, there's a shortcut to stylish e-mails: The subject line can be the e-mail message. Yes, it's true! Very sharply written subject lines are marvelous time-savers but you must put "(EOM)"—that is, end of message—at the end or else we'll be opening up the mail and discovering a blank space. (Now we're back to time-suck.)

They never send chain letters or other dumb stuff by e-mail.

Does that sound harsh? Good. Maybe you'll listen.

E-mails Can Be Dangerous

One of the secrets of modern life is knowing how to handle technology. Some call it "high tech with warm touch." E-mails can be very challenging, especially for people who haven't mastered some of the cardinal rules. Here goes:

Cardinal Rule 1: E-mails are written and read in a vacuum. Sarcasm rarely works unless accompanied by an emoticon. And even then . . .

Cardinal Rule 2: The subject line is critically important. It must be provocative, hard to ignore, compelling.

Cardinal Rule 3: E-mails are more permanent than a stamped letter. Even after you delete an e-mail, it's still floating around in cyberspace.

Cardinal Rule 4: Alert your reader to an e-mail's length and urgency, right at the top.

Cardinal Rule 5: Attitude counts and comes through in an e-mail. One-word responses come across as brusque. They might be easy for the writer, but for the reader . . . *ugh*.

Cardinal Rule 6: When you mention a Web site address, include the link in your message so your recipient can navigate to the site.

Cardinal Rule 7: Don't spam your database-of-present-and-future-contacts with stupid jokes and nonsensical information. Future employers are looking for evidence that you're proactive and are not going to waste company time.

Cardinal Rule 8: Don't react . . . to minor irritations, to clueless behavior, to dumb decisions by others. Don't send that e-mail.

Cardinal Rule 9: Add a signature line to all of your e-mails that includes name, company, e-mail address, and phone number. Four lines, maximum. If you can, adding a dollop of color to your company name adds a little flair.

They do not make appointments by e-mail.

My God, woman, reel it in. *"They do not make appointments by e-mail?"* How in heaven's name do you make appointments? You pick up the phone and you do it in real time! There's way too much time being wasted with the back and forth . . . a phone call with calendars at the ready? Beautiful.

They use spell- and grammar-check.

In the excitement of the instantaneous letter (a.k.a. an e-mail), some people have been known to take liberties with mundane things like grammar and spelling. After all, these short little missives are of no consequence, or so they think. (Of course, they think wrong.) We may not say it but we all think it: Sloppy e-mails are symptomatic of your lack of professionalism. Yes, it means working a little harder and perhaps even going to dictionary.com in the middle of a sentence, but that's what the fabulous do. (Caveat: Even spell-check gets it wrong. Read your work!)

They are explicit to avoid confusion.

There is no tone to an e-mail. That's right, no tone. E-mails operate in a vacuum, so even though you think you're being funny, I might not get it. That's why God invented emoticons. Now, I'll admit, you can't use emoticons everywhere . . . a little smiley face on a note to your boss might not go over big. That's also why you must never be smug or arch, much as you'd like to.

They close the loop.

If you're handing out your e-mail address, you are now accountable, which means you have entered into an implied agreement to read and respond to your e-mails in a timely fashion. Don't leave us hanging. Please, send a short message letting us know you're in receipt of our missive. If you're off e-mail due to travel or looming deadlines, inform your database that you will not be reading e-mails until a determined date.

They reference previous e-mail.

This is how the truly fabulous earn their stripes—they never make you sweat or look clueless. They don't want you to work that hard. Whether it's a cut-and-paste of your previous e-mails or restating the question/problems right at the top, the fabulous bring you up to date so you can give a well-informed response.

They suspend work-related e-mails on the weekend.

There's a good reason our nerves are frayed, our tempers are short, and we're overwhelmed: weekend e-mails. Unless it's urgent, wait for Monday morning.

VOICEMAILS

They never leave a voicemail message that's more than 20 seconds long.

A proper voicemail is quite simple: your name, your phone number, and a short explanation or purpose for the call.

Don't just sit there. Pick up the phone or write a note, and celebrate someone's good fortune!

DEF
3
2
1
4
7
PRS
8
TUV
9
WXY
0

Please Pick Up the Phone!

I mean it. Let's not make e-mail messages our solo form of communication. There are limits to e-mail. A thank-you note, for example. After I spent hours scouring the stores looking for that perfect gift, please don't send me a "heartfelt" e-mail of thanks. Buy a box of note cards. Skip the boilerplate and let me know how you appreciate my thoughtfulness. Write it by hand in your best handwriting. Affix the stamp and send it. I'll probably save it and think of you with great affection.

Please call me when you hear or wish to share good news. An e-mail is fine but don't underestimate how much a phone call can accomplish. Not only can we revel in the happy moment but perhaps we can brainstorm even bigger opportunities.

Please call me when something comes across your desk and you think of me. Not only will I be flattered but I will use the phone call to demonstrate my interest in *your* success. Both of us will hang up the phone feeling good that we're rooting for one another.

Please don't worry about interrupting me. If I'm in the middle of something, I'll tell you right away and promise to call you back at a mutually convenient time. I know that's the reason most people use e-mails to correspond, but we're missing opportunities to know one another on a very deep and satisfying level. Don't be afraid to express your feelings and move the relationship into a more intimate mode.

Please call me but when you do, leave your name and phone number. Don't rush this part on the message—take your time. And remember to keep the voicemail messages to the point and save the stream-of-consciousness thoughts for your blog entries.

Please call during regular business hours. You may be wide-awake at two o'clock in the morning but frankly, a ringing cell phone at that hour is quite alarming. And unnecessary.

Notes are nice but sometimes only a call will do. Capiche?

Repeat the phone number a second time if you're an unfamiliar voice to the person you're calling. That's it. Does it shock you to know that some people (okay, me!) listen to the first five seconds of a voicemail and then delete the message before getting to the end?

They do not slur their name or phone number.

Practice, people, practice. Take a nice, deep breath and then say your name and your phone number slowly and clearly, so the receiver can write it down.

HANDWRITTEN NOTES

Pity the stationers who once could count on some business. In the good old days, people ordered personal note cards and used them to convey heartfelt appreciation, condolences, and congratulations—by mail.

Guess what? The good old days are still here, especially for the fabulous types who want to leave nothing to chance (especially their reputation for making the extra effort to delight someone with their appreciation).

While there's a lot to be said for e-mail and its efficiency, it simply does not create the "wow" that occurs when a handwritten note arrives in the mail. There's something so deliciously old fashioned and gracious about seeing someone's handwriting on an envelope and knowing that they took that extra step to express their feelings. And that's why you should never miss the opportunity to send a handwritten note! It not only sets you apart (differentiation is the name of the game); it also conveys self-assurance and a huge dollop of panache.

They know the secret to a well-written thank-you note.

Pssst. I'm about to share one of the secrets of the universe: how to write an excellent thank-you note. This secret has been handed down generation by generation but somehow missed the current generation, which thinks it's totally cool to just text a thank-you note for an interview, *from the elevator,* en route home from the meeting.

Nope, not happening. The secret to a well-written thank-you note is to, first of all, be sincere. Or funny. Or ironic. But spell the person's name correctly. That always helps.

Let them know why you're writing: to express sympathies, gratitude, congratulations, or maybe to accompany a check for the money you owe them. Perhaps a line or two about how you're faring, then right to the closing lines. Take your pick: "Again, my sincerest condolences," "We're thrilled for you!" or "The chicken cutlets were good." Then, you're ready to give the closer that feels most comfortable, such as "Warmest regards" or "Sincerely" or "Very Truly Yours." You want to sign "Love always"? Go right ahead, but only if you're not writing to your former high school boyfriend, who still wants to know why you broke up with him.

They don't use the love stamp unless they're getting married.

Genius is in the details and that is why the U.S. Postal Service offers choices for snail mail. I'm quite familiar with the LOVE stamp, though I would hesitate to use it. Even if it were the only stamp available to me, I would probably send up a smoke signal rather than confuse the reader with my heart's intentions.

They give good text.

While e-mail is the communication medium for practically everyone, here's a fascinating fact to mull over: It's so old to e-mail. Most young people prefer text messages to their phone. If you're trying to reach someone thirty years old and younger, and think you have the wrong e-mail address, listen up: Forget the e-mail and write them a text message. But once again, make sure the message is well constructed with attention to spelling and grammar. Newsflash: Badly constructed text messages can undermine your authority and credibility.

And finally, I'm gonna state the obvious: Lots of people enjoy spending their evening hours doing dumb and mundane things like reading, laundry, and dreaming up brilliant but cockamamie, never-to-see-the-light-of-day projects, which is why it's rude to call or text message someone after nine o'clock in the evening (unless of course it's an emergency) with your *brilliant* idea. How can I put it gently? Leave us alone!

WANT TO GO FOR IT?

To be utterly and completely bewitching, both virtually and in person:

1. **Don't rush for the bottom line.** In your eagerness to move things off your plate, don't send brusque communiqués that can be interpreted as harsh or cold. Always begin a missive with a warm salutatory greeting and introductory sentence. One-word or two-word responses ("sure" and "got it") come across as snarky and can be disconcerting to the reader.

2. **Take pride in everything that has your name attached.** That means ruthless editing (or at least, making sure

you keep spell- and grammar-checking your copy). If your e-mail server doesn't offer those screening measures and you're prone to spelling "separately" as "seperetely," write the copy on a document page, proof it, and then cut and paste.

3. **Do not overuse virtual communication and exclude other forms.** Yes, I know, e-mail is terrifically efficient and, my God, how did we live without text messaging, but we're paying a psychic price if we forget how much fun a phone call in real time can be (or how effective). Mix and match virtual communications so that you're always using the mode of communication that's most effective and relevant to what you're trying to accomplish. And remember to always infuse every call or message with the same warm and clever persona you'd offer in a face-to-face meeting.

4. **Want to blow someone's mind?** If you do get rejected for a job, send a handwritten thank-you note acknowledging the interviewer for the opportunity to meet. That's right: rejected! The guy that got the position could be toast in thirty days and guess who might get a call for another meeting?

RESOURCES

When I realize I need to brush up on my grammar *and* my online jargon I turn to:

Send: Why People Email So Badly and How to Do It Better **by David Shipley and Will Schwalbe**

Shipley, David, and Will Schwalbe. *Send: Why People Email So Badly and How to Do It Better.*
New York: Alfred A. Knopf, 2008.

Just because we have access to e-mail doesn't mean we know how to write terrific e-mail messages, or know when to forget e-mail and just pick up the phone. In the last ten years, our correspondence habits have changed drastically. Where we once would have waited for a response, we now expect a response to come instantaneously. Where we once would have written a heartfelt note of appreciation or condolence, we now write three bland sentences and hit the "Send" button. Buy this book in bulk and send it all the people in your life who leave the subject line *blank* (you're going to omit the headline to your missive?) and then get mad because you leave their e-mails for last.

www.netlingo.com
The definitive guide to "get with the program." All the abbreviations and slang you need to show the reader that you're with-it.

Essentials of English: A Practical Handbook Covering All the Rules of English Grammar and Writing Style
by Vincent Hopper et al.

Hopper, Vincent, et al. *Essentials of English: A Practical Handbook Covering All the Rules of English Grammar and Writing Style.* New York: Barron's Educational Series, 1990.

Whether you communicate by text messaging, insta-messaging, e-mail, or snail mail, you ought to have a primer for those moments when trying to decide: Should I *italicize* or underline The New Yorker (either one is appropriate, depending on the context). And that's another thing I need to work on: Does the period go inside the parenthesis or outside of the parenthesis? Hmmm . . .

ONE WAY

Fabulous people have a board.

When socialite Sandy Hill Pittman climbed Mt. Everest, she brought along an espresso machine. She also brought along a sherpa or two to carry it. (Really, who wouldn't want a cup of espresso after making camp on a frigid, death-inviting mountain?)

Take it from Sandy, who was once considered fabulous (but was later banished from the poached salmon circuit for her unwillingness to sacrifice her espresso), it's good to have a sherpa: a person to give advice and support, and carry some weight (or in her case, short-rope you up the mountain), as you make the slow but absolutely guaranteed climb to the top.

WHERE TO START:

A sherpa to schlep an espresso machine is rather brilliant (in a selfish, self-indulgent sort of way), but is it enough? More than just a sherpa, perhaps you need a board of directors?

Treasure those who green-light your dreams.

If you lead a full, busy life . . . with friendships that sometimes go awry . . . with business problems that can't be discussed with anyone you work with . . . with family issues that need a soulful ear and big shoulders . . . if over the last six months you've laid in bed at night staring at the ceiling with a problem that really should be inconsequential ("How come I wasn't invited to so-and-so's party?") but has morphed into something that just won't go away ("Was it because I forgot to tell so-and-so that I had the new phone number of the genius colorist who left the salon and moved to the city?") . . . if you've ever felt alone with your neuroses, your phobias, and the weight of the world on your shoulders . . . *yes, you need a board.*

A board is a group of individuals who may not know one another but know *you,* and who are willing to put their brains and their expertise at your disposal for however long you need it. You do not need consensus from the board nor do all members need to weigh in and advise on all matters, but you *do* need members to whom you can give your complete trust. The purpose of a personal board is to enable you to get to the answer or the decision that makes you feel ready to take the next step.

WHO SERVES ON YOUR BOARD?

No two boards are alike. That's the glory of it all—you get to choose who you want to advise you, based on the kind of advice you're looking for.

My board has to close the gap that stands between me and my shifting array of ambitions and goals. My board offers fashion and style advice, parenting suggestions, common sense, new business brainstorming, editorial support, therapeutic interventions, and most importantly, the definitive answers for all of my etiquette blind spots. And should I come upon someone with extraordinary talents who likes offering advice (and is not hurt when it's not followed verbatim), I'll invite them to serve, too. Do I have a big board? Yes and no, because I use their time discriminately (as you should, too).

If you're lucky, you already know one or two people who are committed to you and your success. If you don't, stop whatever it is you are doing and start building bridges to talented, soulfully intelligent, and energetic people, and cultivate them as board members in training. Make sure they know you're willing, eager, and qualified to serve on their board, too.

I've seen it first hand. When the going gets tough, the smartest get going by reaching out to a handpicked group of advisors who will roll up their sleeves and get the Fabulous One back on her launch pad.

With the board's backing, you will be able to get the right kind of feedback (honest and supportive), see the big picture (perspective, perspective, perspective), plot and connive with the help of master strategists, and feel empowered by the nurturing and the prodding of people who wish you well.

Now let's look at how your guides are gonna short-rope *you* up the mountain.

SELECTING YOUR BOARD

A good board cares about your success.

Besides smarts and savvy, a board member has to have the confidence to see you accomplish your goals. These are the people who never worry that someone will have a bigger job or

How to Give Honest Feedback

There comes a time when everyone thinks out loud, trying to figure out why things are not going well. If this "discovery" phase takes place within earshot of a board member, it is the board member's responsibility to ask permission to share an insight that might shed some light.

It is only during this "trying to figure it out" phase that maximum insight can be achieved. Believe me, do not try to offer constructive feedback or sincere advice when someone is down on his luck or up with euphoria—at those times, our ears simply don't work.

The other trick to giving feedback is how you say it. Asking permission is the only acceptable entry point and should it be denied, the feedback must be held back, perhaps indefinitely. If permission has been granted, start the conversation by stating the listener's best assets. Reiterate once again your complete and total commitment to their happiness and achievement even while they protest, "It's okay, get right to the point." Do not listen. Under no circumstances should you get right to the point.

Now, with dulcet tones, share your observation and assure your friend that this minor flaw is just a blip, a minor imperfection in someone whose entire life has been devoted to being the best they can be. Only share one shortcoming at a time. Let your words sink in but do not try to dilute their impact. You said what you needed to say. Now your friend must do their part and see if your comments do apply. Do not rush to change the subject . . . let the friend control the remainder of the conversation. (It's also good to have a doctor's appointment that can't be missed.)

a swankier kitchen—they just love seeing people get what they deserve. A board member who is that loyal will not abandon you when you're down. They won't screen your phone calls or pretend they're out of town. On the contrary, the minute you ask for help they're thumbing through their contact list to get you the support you need. So do not take the selection of a board member lightly and do not second-guess yourself. In the words of Antoine Saint-Exupery in *The Little Prince* (kudos: Aunt Eddy), "It is only with the heart that one can see rightly. What is essential is invisible to the eye." *You* know who is rooting for you.

A good board sees the big picture.

Good board members don't live in a vacuum. They understand the stakes of living a full and complete life. So they will never ask something of you that they wouldn't ask of themselves. Having said that, they also don't get trapped in emotional quicksand when it comes to decision making. This is why a board is so important—without baggage and laundry and back stories to muddy the picture, they can listen and advise and get you to understand what's really important.

A good board member is self-aware.

Serving on someone's board requires a keen knowledge of one's own talents and limitations. Great board members will not hesitate to offer advice if it falls under their purview but they will never grope in the dark. The point of serving on a board is to support and assist, not to meddle or mess things up. They don't need to have all the answers (no one does) but it's helpful if they're the types who know where and how to get the information that will resolve the question.

A good board takes you and your travails seriously.

It is so easy to get balled up about nothing. Don't we all have moments when we think, "This is gonna cost me my job?" Haven't we all been sick with worry about a routine blood test or a baby's hacking cough? It's easy to get lost and frightened and blow things out of proportion when it's you all alone, conjuring up these "what if" scenarios and playing out a hundred different outcomes, most of them dire. But when you have people around you who will look at all your options and stand by you as you make the choices that are smart and sensible, well, then the anxiety lessens and you can move up the mountain with the confidence you'll need to scale the big heights.

Look, leading a big, full, ambitious life is a lot like climbing a really big mountain. You never look to the top. After all, what could be more daunting than imagining the tough, scary, and unpredictable climb? Well, that's pretty much what we all do every day. We start at the bottom and make our way up. And if we're really lucky, we have friends and colleagues who understand how to make the climb an absolute blast.

A good board loves you enough to tell you the truth.

Don't you think people would be less irritating and annoying if they had more honest (and loving) feedback?

I think so. I think some people are blithely unaware of how they are perceived. It's not easy to tell someone that they sound like a blowhard or that their laugh comes across as shrill and insincere. Believe me, no one relishes the idea of telling someone that they're not included in social functions because they're haughty and arrogant. But, we must expect our board members to be forthright with us at the opportune moment or schedule a chat and say, "May I share something with you that I'm seeing?" and then lay it right on the line. And when this happens, we have to be ready to listen and know that if there's truth to what our board member is saying, we've got to put that information to work (immediately!) because we've selected our board members for their loyalty and eagle-eyed observations (and because they believe in us).

WORKING WITH YOUR BOARD

Stack your board with competence.

A good board has to be privy to your biggest dreams. They can't possibly want to achieve your goals as much as you do, but they have to want you to nail it. So don't put on a front or pretend things are better than they seem. Surround yourself with people who believe in you more than you believe in yourself and occasionally (and when necessary) let them drag you across the finish line.

Try to find members with different interests and talents. Someone who's savvy about marketing will be able to help you position yourself both professionally and socially; a member who's also a good writer will be able to review your resumé or cover letter or help you freshen up your e-mails so that they are more entertaining as well as informative. Look for a member who understands the way business works and by that I mean knows where to go to get information on salary, bonuses, and other perks you can negotiate for when landing a plummy job. Remember, your board is there to close the gap on areas of knowledge and expertise where you feel you need shoring up.

To encourage your board's buy-in, let them know what's going on in your life. If your climb has been postponed by a change in management, the board needs to know this. If you've been short-listed for a top position or interviewed for a magazine story, they need to know this. Think of your board as a group of doting aunts who can never tire of hearing about your latest and most exciting exploits. There's a very fine line between bragging and keeping your board up to date, but you need to master that line because board members can be effective viral marketers for the people they champion.

A board member's time must never be wasted.

Use your board's time wisely. Go ahead and pick their pretty/handsome brains but know in advance what you're looking for. Remember, these high-performers are doing all this scheming and strategizing *free of charge* so be respectful of their acumen and don't waste their brainpower with nonsense. Whenever there's an opportunity to show your appreciation (handwritten note, anyone?) for God's sake, go for it!

Keep your board in the loop.

Your board members should be kept fully updated on matters where they have been consulted. Let them know what's working and what isn't . . . don't be afraid to share the temporary roadblocks and segues. Be effusively appreciative—notes, calls, vintage hankies—along with briefer e-mails with late-breaking information. What you must never do is drop the ball entirely (i.e., ask for support/advice and then forget that they might be interested to see how their advice/support made a difference).

Your Board of Directors

You know what it's like: You have to make a decision about your business, your job, or family life, or maybe you just need some feedback on the way you're approaching the world. You make a mental list of the people that you can call and, frankly, everyone is so busy! (I can't figure out what we used to do with all the time that we used to have. Did everyone *knit*?)

Who do you call?

If you're lucky, you have one or two people who can help you see the glimmer of truth you're searching for. And if you're in the *stratosphere* as far as luck is concerned, you have a team of advisors, a virtual "board of directors," to offer you support, advice, strategy, and connections.

Everyone should have a board. And here's why:

A board (*your board*) champions your growth and your power. With a board backing you, you can make tough decisions. You can go out on a limb. You can push through the barriers that might be holding you back. A board can steer you in the right direction when you've lost your road map.

A good board must include people with common sense. Never underestimate the joy of spending time with someone who can see the big picture instead of retreating to myopia. It's also wise to staff your board with master strategists who know where to pull the levers and people who don't keep score—that is, who tend to give rather than take. These nurturing souls are standouts when you're in a crux and need immediate assistance. And find people who know how to laugh.

Imagine your life with a board that backs you completely because they think you're the greatest. Imagine surrounding yourself with believers who have talents you can tap when you need them. Imagine not having to go through the tough days of work and life alone. Now, you can do anything!

Encourage the board to hold you accountable.

A board that is empowered to hold you accountable to the highest of standards is not going to let you take the path of least resistance. They know what you are capable of. They know what you can accomplish.

The board serves many roles, but for most of us the board's chief function is to help us believe in ourselves. It's easy to give up, shrug, and rationalize a decision that seems safe in the short run. It's hard to keep challenging ourselves and dreaming up bigger goals, but the board doesn't doubt us the way we doubt ourselves. The board is supremely confident that we can do it, and sometimes that's all we need to convince *ourselves*.

Keep all of your relationships symmetrical—crow about your board to your network and look for opportunities to get your members in front of the influentials that you know. To get the most out of your board, you have to believe in them as much as they believe in you.

WANT TO GO FOR IT?

To create a versatile, vibrant, remarkable band of believers who won't stop until you're at the top:

1. **Identify people who are high energy and like to wave the pompoms.** Select board members who love collaboration and cooperation and have the ego-strength to see someone accomplish big things.

2. **Value common sense.** While I'm all for choosing members who are experts in their field, there's a lot to be said for stacking the board with Grandma Sally types who may not have had the advantage of a formal

education but are so steeped in common sense that they're the first person you can talk to when you need some perspective.

3. **Look for a great sense of humor and an ability to make you laugh at yourself.** This is non-negotiable. Send the deadly serious and earnest types to someone else's board (like your frenemy's, perhaps?)

RESOURCES

You think it's easy trying to identify the smartest people in the room?

Pride and Prejudice by Jane Austen

Austen, Jane. *Pride and Prejudice.*
New York: Signet Classic, 1813.

Trying to find a guide to selecting a board member? Why not read the greatest writer on sage wisdom and human folly? What didn't we learn about human nature by this most perfect novel?

Never Eat Alone: And Other Secrets to Success, One Relationship at a Time by Keith Ferrazzi

Ferrazzi, Keith. *Never Eat Alone: And Other Secrets to Success, One Relationship at a Time.*
New York: Doubleday, 2005.

How do you get in front of the right people? Isn't that what everybody wants to know? According to Ferrazzi, the secret to access is relationships—connecting on a meaningful level with the kinds of people that can green-light an idea or set up a meeting that can lead to an opportunity. And how do you do that? You cultivate a cadre of allies, supporters, champions, mentors, advisors, and consultants who believe that everyone should get a nice-sized slice of a very nice pie.

Let Us Praise . . .

Yes, life is cuckoo. Would we want it any other way? Too many phone calls to return, too many e-mails to sift through, yet in the midst of our delirium at life's crazy pace, let us **celebrate** those who:

- eschewed multitasking when on the phone
- returned our calls within twenty-four hours
- got to the point when leaving a voicemail
- attached documents when they referred to the documents
- used e-mail to engage and delight us at the same time they answered our questions or discussed an issue
- flagged the subject line to alert us to the time-sensitivity of the message
- spell-checked their missives
- sent a note by snail mail, and
- for good measure, threw in some punctuation

Let us **rejoice** in those who:

- took the role of "host" at social functions and introduced people with vivacity and enthusiasm to get the conversation rolling
- looked us straight in the eye when conversing rather than searching the room looking for someone more important

- kept the cell phone on mute to ensure that our conversation was uninterrupted

- took being present seriously

- had the confidence to admit when they didn't know something

- went to dinner on a Saturday night without the BlackBerry, since everyone knows that rarely does anyone get e-mail of consequence on a Saturday night

Let us **praise** those who:

- praised us

- gave referrals

- made recommendations

- championed others without asking for anything in return

- showed up for work/play/life with enthusiasm even when they had a lousy night's sleep, lost money in the stock market, or missed the final episode of *Lost*

- never tired of expressing support and encouragement

- wished us well

- made us feel good about ourselves

Conclusion

To the Readers Who Put Up With My Rants:

By this point, you have either come to the conclusion that I'm a control freak and obsessive about thank-you notes, or you feel like you've met your kindred spirit. In either case, you are right. When it comes to a polished presentation, I am a bit obsessive about, well, everything. I've written the book about it because **everything matters.**

Paying attention to everything is how you become fabulous. Paying heed to the shine of your shoes, knowing when to stop e-mailing and pick up the phone, turning off the BlackBerry when you're at a wedding (unless of course you're Dr. Mehmet Oz and waiting to hear if Oprah is renewing your contract and, oh yes, whether that guy in ICU had to be resuscitated), finding the purpose to your life, eliciting advice, giving of yourself to everyone. This is also how you maintain fabulous: by staying relevant, being fun to work with, and as a result, being the last to be pink-slipped. (Face it: How can they live without you?)

A tall order, to be sure. But, look, it's crazy out there. Lots of superbly talented people are being jettisoned, some permanently. Jobs are few and most of them are not even advertised . . . it's all word-of-mouth. If the word-of-mouth on you is ho-hum, boy, are you in for a dry spell. Having a persona that's sizzling with brio and full engagement is not just an iPhone with apps—that is, frivolous or a nice thing to have. It's a necessity. It's like air.

For a long time being okay was good enough, but not now. For those of us who have always reveled in outperforming the competition, it's finally our time. It's *your* time, if you're willing to shore up your confidence, brush up on your manners, and create a first impression that leaves little doubt that you're truly extraordinary. The places you'll go and the people you'll meet when you're buoyant with optimism—I get goose bumps just thinking about how your life will be enhanced!

Remember this: No one climbs Mt. Everest by themselves. They have helpers and schleppers, and maybe even people who lug espresso machines. Don't take this board of directors thing too lightly, because even if you're not planning to climb a mountain, you're always going to need people around you that really care about you and your happiness. When things go awry, this handpicked group of advisors is going to get you back on your feet and keep reminding you of what you've done and who you are and how you're going to do it again. Surround yourself with friends and allies who are ready and willing to listen empathically, make a call, or set up an introduction. It's not just a nice thing to have. Like panache, having support is a requirement. It's like air.

It doesn't happen overnight. No one can possibly assemble an advisory board, a classic wardrobe, and a shoe polishing kit in one night—but it doesn't matter. Take little steps . . .

Start smiling for no reason. Then, introduce yourself to a stranger. Initiate a handshake instead of holding back and waiting for someone to introduce themselves to you. Make sure the subject line of your e-mail intrigues the reader with your originality and verve. And change that sound loop inside your head until you're listening to nonstop and ridiculously sublime commentary that makes you feel like you can take on the world.

Why not? You've got something better to do?

Book Shopping List

The Art of Mingling: Easy, Fun, and Proven Techniques for Mastering Any Room.
Martinet, Jeanne.
New York: St. Martin's Griffin, 2006.

The Barefoot Contessa Cookbook.
Garten, Ina.
New York: Clarkson Potter/Publisher, 1999.

The Big Sister's Guide to the World of Work: The Inside Rules Every Working Girl Must Know.
DiFalco, Marcelle Langan, and Jocelyn Greenky Herz.
New York: Fireside, 2005.

Brag! The Art of Tooting Your Own Horn.
Klaus, Peggy.
New York: Warner Business Books, 2003.

D.V.
Vreeland, Diana.
New York: Alfred A. Knopf, Inc., 1984.

Do One Nice Thing: Little Things You Can Do to Make the World a Lot Nicer.
Tenzer, Debbie.
New York: Crown Publishers, 2009.

Eccentric Glamour: Creating an Insanely More Fabulous You.
Doonan, Simon.
New York: Simon & Schuster Paperbacks, 2008.

Emotional Intelligence: Why It Can Matter More Than IQ.
Goleman, Daniel.
United States: Bantam, 1995.

Essentials of English: A Practical Handbook Covering All the Rules of English Grammar and Writing Style.
Hopper, Vincent, et al.
New York: Barron's Educational Series, 1990.

How to Win Friends and Influence People.
Carnegie, Dale.
New York: Pocket Books, 1936.

The Illustrated Woody Allen Reader.
Allen, Woody.
New York: Alfred A. Knopf, Inc., 1993.

Life Is Short, Wear Your Party Pants.
LaRoche, Loretta.
Carlsbad, CA: Hay House, Inc., 2003.

Masters of Networking: Building Relationships for Your Pocketbook and Soul.
Misner, Ivan, and Don Morgan.
Atlanta: Bard Press, 2000.

Miss Manners' Guide to Excruciatingly Correct Behavior.
Martin, Judith.
New York: W. W. Norton & Company, 2005.

Never Eat Alone: And Other Secrets to Success, One Relationship at a Time.
Ferrazzi, Keith.
New York: Doubleday, 2005.

On Becoming a Leader.
Bennis, Warren.
Reading, MA: Addison-Wesley Publishing Company, Inc., 1989.

The One Hundred: A Guide to the Pieces Every Stylish Woman Must Own.
Garcia, Nina.
New York: HarperCollins Publishers, 2008.

The Power of Nice: How to Conquer the Business World With Kindness.
Kaplan Thaler, Linda, and Robin Koval.
New York: Doubleday, 2006.

Pride and Prejudice.
Austen, Jane.
New York: Signet Classic, 1813.

The Principles of Uncertainty.
Kalman, Maira.
New York: The Penguin Press, 2007.

Rare Bird of Fashion (The Irreverent Iris Apfel).
Boman, Eric.
New York: Thames & Hudson, Inc., 2007.

Send: Why People Email So Badly and How to Do It Better.
Shipley, David, and Will Schwalbe.
New York: Alfred A. Knopf, 2008.

Shakespeare in Charge: The Bard's Guide to Leading and Succeeding on the Business Stage.
Augustine, Norman, and Kenneth Adelman.
New York: Hyperion, 1999.

Wacky Chicks: Life Lessons from Fearlessly Inappropriate and Fabulously Eccentric Women.
Doonan, Simon.
New York: Simon & Schuster, 2003.

The Way We Lived Then: Recollections of a Well-Known Name Dropper.
Dunne, Dominick.
New York: Crown Publishers, 1999.

What to Say When You Talk to Your Self.
Helmstetter, Shad.
New York: Pocket Books, 1982.

What Would Jackie Do? An Inspired Guide to Distinctive Living.
Branch, Shelly, and Sue Callaway.
New York: Gotham Books, 2005.

About Ellen Lubin-Sherman

PHOTO BY SARAH MERIANS

Ellen Lubin-Sherman got her start in business feeding gossip items to Liz Smith, the esteemed former gossip columnist at the *New York Daily News.* Those early days of name-dropping were the perfect foundation for her later work in cultivating and branding identities for some of the country's most luxurious products. Today she uses that expertise to coach corporations and business leaders in the art of creating a polished presentation.

After earning her undergraduate degree in communications and then a master's degree from the Medill School of Journalism (Northwestern University, Evanston, IL), Ellen went to work for some of NYC's top communications firms, advising top-tier brands including The Gap, Perrier Water, and Martha Stewart. In 1998 Ellen started her own company, specializing in brand awareness for lifestyle and beauty products.

Four years later Ellen repositioned her eponymous company to become LAUNCH, a coaching and consulting firm for business leaders and corporations who need to craft the visuals and the messages that will burnish their reputation as leaders and differentiate them in the marketplace.

Today, in addition to executive coaching and consulting, Ellen is a sought-after speaker for companies and groups that are desperate to know how they can become fabulous.